Vintage Yosemite

Vintage Yosemite

Glass Plate Photographs of Early 20th-Century Yosemite

by Harold A. Taylor

Edited by Robert Elliott and Susan Entsminger

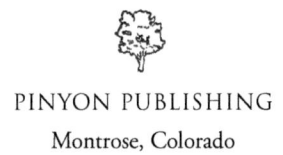

PINYON PUBLISHING
Montrose, Colorado

Copyright © 2022 by Robert Elliott and Susan Entsminger

All rights reserved. Except as permitted under the U.S. Copyright Act of 1976, no part of this publication may be reproduced, distributed, or transmitted in any form or by any means, or stored in a database or retrieval system, without the prior written permission of the publisher, except for brief quotations in articles, books, and reviews.

Cover Art: Harold A. Taylor's *Haymaking Wagon below Yosemite Falls in Cook's Meadow* (503a, 8" x 10") and *Overhanging Rock, Wide Angle (Glacier Point)* (591, 6.5" x 8.5")

Glass Plate Photographs by Harold A. Taylor (ca. 1902-1907). Reference numbers identify the images in the physical and digital archives, in the private collection of Robert Elliott and Susan Entsminger.

Modern images documenting the process of preserving and archiving the glass plates (on pages 139-141) by Robert Elliott and Susan Entsminger

Taylor quotations come from a 1949 letter from Harold Taylor to Yosemite administrator, Ralph Anderson.

Special thanks to Leroy Radanovich for initial scans and commentary.

First Edition: November 2022

Pinyon Publishing
23847 V66 Trail, Montrose, CO 81403
www.pinyon-publishing.com

Library of Congress Control Number: 2022916428
ISBN: 978-1-936671-89-2

For our parents

"I have a very warm spot in my heart for the Valley, and who knows but you might see me in the Valley one of these days."

—Harold A. Taylor (1878-1960)

Contents

Photograph Title (reference number, glass plate dimensions)

Preface xv

Harold A. Taylor in Yosemite 1

   Studio of the Three Arrows (672, 6.5" x 8.5") 2
   Detail of *Studio of the Three Arrows* (672, 6.5" x 8.5") 3

Valley Views

   Entrance to Yosemite, View from Historic Artist Point (627a, 8" x 10") 7
   View from Historic Inspiration Point (537, 8" x 10") 8
   View from Stanford Point (542, 6.5" x 8.5") 9
   View from Moran Point (600, 6.5" x 8.5") 10
   Gates of the Valley, with 9 People in Wagon, 4 horses (679b, 6.5" x 8.5") ... 10
   Gates of the Valley with Merced River and Bridalveil Fall (558a, 6.5" x 8.5") 11
   Gates of the Valley with Merced River and Bridalveil Fall (558b, 6.5" x 8.5") 11
   Gates of the Valley: July 24, 1903 (562, 6.5" x 8.5") 12
   Oak Trees, Yosemite Valley (615, 6.5" x 8.5") 13
   Indian Acorn Cache (531, 8" x 10") 14
   Indian Camp (528, 8" x 10") 15
   Haymaking Wagon below Yosemite Falls in Cook's Meadow (503a, 8" x 10") 16
   Detail of *Haymaking Wagon* (503a, 8" x 10") 17
   Haying Piles Leidig Meadow, Looking West toward Cathedral Rocks (674a, 8" x 10") 17
   Big Cedar Tree (661, 6.5" x 8.5") 18
   Trail through Woods (405, 5" x 7") 19

WATERFALLS

Yosemite Falls from Four Mile Trail to Glacier Point (509, 8" x 10") 23
Yosemite Falls from Four Mile Trail to Glacier Point (509a, 8" x 10")........24
Yosemite Falls from Meadow (510, 6.5" x 8.5") 25
Yosemite Falls Road (Trail) (511, 6.5" x 8.5") 26
Yosemite Falls Road (Trail) (647, 6.5" x 8.5") 27
Upper Yosemite Fall (540, 8" x 10")..28
Yosemite Falls Reflection (613, 8" x 10") 29
Vernal Fall (535, 8" x 10") 30
Nevada Fall (519, 8" x 10") 31
Bridalveil Fall (538, 8" x 10") 32
Bridalveil Fall (650, 6.5" x 8.5") 33
Bridalveil Fall (673, 6.5" x 8.5") 34
Bridalveil Fall (401, 6.5" x 8.5") 35
Cascade Falls (559, 6.5" x 8.5") 36

ROCKS

El Capitan Morning Landscape (539c, 8" x 10")..39
El Capitan Afternoon (586, 6.5" x 8.5")..40
El Capitan Afternoon with Clouds (680, 6.5" x 8.5") 41
Three Brothers, Wide Angle (636, 6.5" x 8.5") 42
Three Brothers (534b, 8" x 10")..43
Three Brothers from the Road (583, 6.5" x 8.5") 44
Washington Column (602, 6.5" x 8.5") 45
North Dome from Happy Isles (597, 6.5" x 8.5").......................................46
North Dome from Happy Isles (637, 6.5" x 8.5").......................................47
North Dome, Royal Arches, and Washington Column (677a, 6.5" x 8.5")..48
Cathedral Spires from River (536b, 8" x 10") 49
Cathedral Spires with Road and Wagon (504, 8" x 10")............................50
Detail of *Cathedral Spires with Road and Wagon* (504, 8" x 10") 50
Cathedral Spires Telephoto (658, 6.5" x 8.5") 51
Taft Point (404, 6.5" x 8.5")..52

Detail of *Taft Point* (404, 6.5" x 8.5") 52
Sentinel Rock (552, 6.5" x 8.5") 53
Sentinel Rock (555, 6.5" x 8.5") 54
Sentinel Rock Profile with Cathedral Rocks in Background (582, 6.5" x 8.5") 55
Sentinel Dome Tree (686, 6.5" x 8.5") 56
Sentinel Dome Tree (687, 6.5" x 8.5") 56
Photographer's Rock, View of Half Dome from Glacier Point (525, 8" x 10") 57
Detail of *Photographer's Rock* (525, 8" x 10") 57
Overhanging Rock, Two Soldiers (Glacier Point) (603, 6.5" x 8.5") 58
Detail of *Overhanging Rock, Two Soldiers* (603, 6.5" x 8.5") 58
Overhanging Rock, Wide Angle (Glacier Point) (591, 6.5" x 8.5") 59
Detail of *Overhanging Rock, Wide Angle* (591, 6.5" x 8.5") 59
Overhanging Rock, Wide Angle (Glacier Point) (684, 6.5" x 8.5") 60
Detail of *Overhanging Rock, Wide Angle* (684, 6.5" x 8.5") 60
Half Dome from Glacier Point (590, 6.5" x 8.5") 61
Tis-sa-ack, The Great Half Dome, from Washburn Point (683a, 6.5" x 8.5") 62
Half Dome from Glacier Point Trail (581, 6.5" x 8.5") 63
Glacier Point Panorama (685, 6.5" x 8.5") 63
Tenaya Canyon, Early Morning (653, 6.5" x 8.5") 64
Half Dome from Meadow (526, 8" x 10") 64
Half Dome and River (649, 6.5" x 8.5") 65
Half Dome from Bridge (665, 6.5" x 8.5") 66
Half Dome from the Head of Tenaya Canyon (601, 6.5" x 8.5") 67
Mt. Conness and Tenaya Lake (606, 6.5" x 8.5") 67
Tenaya Lake and Cathedral Peak (608, 6.5" x 8.5") 68

LAKES, RIVERS, AND STREAMS

Tenaya Lake Showing Clouds Rest (548, 6.5" x 8.5") 71
Tenaya Lake from Northeast Shore (607, 6.5" x 8.5") 71
Tenaya Creek Study with Bridge (655, 6.5" x 8.5") 72

Tenaya Creek Study (549, 6.5" x 8.5")..73
Creek Study (619, 6.5" x 8.5")..74
Mirror Lake, Showing Road (545, 6.5" x 8.5")..75
Mirror Lake Landscape (598, 6.5" x 8.5")..75
Mirror Lake with Reflection of Mt. Watkins (403, 5" x 7")............................76
Domes from Rocky Point, Leafy Bower (506a, 6.5" x 8.5")..............................77
Lost Arrow Trail, Yosemite Creek (529, 8" x 10")..77
The Bank of the Stream (544b, 8" x 10")...78
Stream Bank (654, 6.5" x 8.5")..79
Meeting of the Waters, Happy Isles, High Water (656, 6.5" x 8.5").............80
Meeting of the Waters, Happy Isles, Low Water (594, 6.5" x 8.5").............80
Merced River with Cathedral Rocks and Spires (554, 6.5" x 8.5")................81
Merced River from El Capitan Bridge (541, 8" x 10")....................................82
Merced River from El Capitan Bridge, Low Water (546, 6.5" x 8.5")........83
Crescent Lake, East of Wawona (620, 6.5" x 8.5")...84
Crescent Lake, East of Wawona (623, 6.5" x 8.5")...85
Minnow Lake with Pink Mimulus *(Monkey-flower), East of Wawona*
  (621, 6.5" x 8.5")..85

SEQUOIAS

Grizzly Giant Base with Ranger (1510, 6.5" x 8.5")..89
Grizzly Giant Base with Carriage and Ranger (1576, 6.5" x 8.5")...............90
Detail of *Grizzly Giant Base with Carriage and Ranger* (1576, 6.5" x 8.5")
 90
Grizzly Giant with Roosevelt Party (1504, 6.5" x 8.5")..................................91
Grizzly Giant (1530, 6.5" x 8.5")..92
Grizzly Giant with Camera Stand (1532, 6.5" x 8.5")....................................93
Grizzly Giant with Ranger at Base (1508, 6.5" x 8.5")...................................94
Grizzly Giant Trunk with Fence (1531, 6.5" x 8.5").......................................95
Fallen Monarch with Stairs, Carriage, and People (15XX, 6.5" x 8.5").....96
Detail of *Fallen Monarch with Stairs, Carriage, and People*
  (15XX, 6.5" x 8.5")...96
Fallen Monarch with Carriage (1503, 6.5" x 8.5")..97

Fallen Monarch (1525, 6.5" x 8.5") 97
Wawona Tree with Carriage and Ranger (1521, 6.5" x 8.5") 98
Detail of *Wawona Tree with Carriage and Ranger* (1521, 6.5" x 8.5")......98
Wawona Tree with Carriage (1554, 6.5" x 8.5") 99
Detail of *Wawona Tree with Carriage* (1554, 6.5" x 8.5")........................99
Vermont and Wawona Trees (1555, 6.5" x 8.5")....................................100
Vermont and Wawona Trees with Rider (1519, 6.5" x 8.5") 101
Detail of *Vermont and Wawona Trees with Rider* (1519, 6.5" x 8.5") 101
Vermont and Wawona Trees, Road Study (1556, 6.5" x 8.5") 102
Vermont Tree, Road Study (1557, 6.5" x 8.5") 103
Old Cabin in Grove (1515, 6.5" x 8.5")..104
Detail of *Old Cabin in Grove* (1515, 6.5" x 8.5") 104
Old Cabin in Grove (1522b, 6.5" x 8.5")..105
Detail of *Old Cabin in Grove* (1522b, 6.5" x 8.5") 105
Cabin in Grove (1522a, 6.5" x 8.5") 106
Cabin in Grove with Carriage (1542, 6.5" x 8.5")..................................107
Detail of *Cabin in Grove with Carriage* (1542, 6.5" x 8.5") 107
Cabin in Grove with Man (1543, 6.5" x 8.5").......................................108
Detail of *Cabin in Grove with Man* (1543, 6.5" x 8.5").........................108
Cabin in Grove, Fallen Tree with Stairs (1541, 6.5" x 8.5")....................109
Haverford and Ohio Trees with View of Cabins (1539, 6.5" x 8.5") 110
Detail of *Haverford and Ohio Trees with View of Cabins* (1539, 6.5" x 8.5") 110
Governor Tree with Man (1536, 6.5" x 8.5") 111
Detail of *Governor Tree with Man* (1536, 6.5" x 8.5") 111
Governor and Commissioners Trees with Man (1538, 6.5" x 8.5") 112
Detail of *Governor and Commissioners Trees with Man* (1538, 6.5" x 8.5") 112
Governor and Commissioners Trees (1537, 6.5" x 8.5")..........................113
Governor Gene Todd Group (1524b, 6.5" x 8.5")..................................114
Governor Gene Todd Group with Carriage (1547, 6.5" x 8.5") 115
Detail of *Governor Gene Todd Group with Carriage* (1547, 6.5" x 8.5") 115
Governor Gene Todd Group with Carriage (1524a, 6.5" x 8.5") 116
Detail of *Governor Gene Todd Group with Carriage* (1524a, 6.5" x 8.5") 116

Bachelor and Three Graces (1527, 6.5" x 8.5") 117
Bachelor and Three Graces with Lady (1505, 6.5" x 8.5") 118
Detail of *Bachelor and Three Graces with Lady* (1505, 6.5" x 8.5") 118
Bachelor and Three Graces (1528, 6.5" x 8.5") 119
Confederate Group and Telescope Tree (1552, 6.5" x 8.5") 120
Confederate Group, Rear View (1551, 6.5" x 8.5") 121
William McKinley Group (1548, 6.5" x 8.5") 121
Columbia and Massachusetts (1546, 6.5" x 8.5") 122
Galen Clark (1559, 6.5" x 8.5") 123
Detail of *Galen Clark* (1559, 6.5" x 8.5") 123
The Old Guard (1545, 6.5" x 8.5") 124
San Diego (1517, 6.5" x 8.5") 125
Most Perfect Tree, Alabama (1534, 6.5" x 8.5") 126
California (1506, 6.5" x 8.5") 127
Hawaiian Islands (1558, 6.5" x 8.5") 128
Faithful Couple (1533, 6.5" x 8.5") 129
Sunset Tree (1535, 6.5" x 8.5") 130
Longfellow and Whittier with Carriage (1553, 6.5" x 8.5") 131
Detail of *Longfellow and Whittier with Carriage* (1553, 6.5" x 8.5") 131
Sequoia Road Study (1549, 6.5" x 8.5") 132
Sequoia Road Study, Diamond Group (1560, 6.5" x 8.5") 133
Sequoia Road Study (1550, 6.5" x 8.5") 133
Lower Grove Road (1529, 6.5" x 8.5") 134
Dead and Living Among the Big Trees (1544, 6.5" x 8.5") 135
The Base of a Sequoia (1540, 6.5" x 8.5") 136
Among Giants (1526, 6.5" x 8.5") 137

Preserving Glass Plate Negatives 139
Bibliography 143
Index 145

PREFACE

In 1878, Harold A. Taylor was born in Croydon, a growing town in south London. In 1896, he left England and settled in Bakersfield, California.

From 1902-1907, Taylor photographed Yosemite, operating out of his Studio of the Three Arrows in Yosemite Valley.

In 1912, Taylor moved to Coronado, where he lived, worked in photography, and established the Coronado Floral Association with his wife Maud. When he started retiring, Harold and Maud moved to El Cajon where they cultivated a half-acre Victorian flower garden on their dear little hill, "Lomita Querida." He died in 1960 at the age of 81.

Taylor gave many of his glass plate negatives to his photographic business partner, William T. Elliott. William later gave the Yosemite and California Missions collections to his son Robert Elliott, who lived near Yosemite from 1971-2015. Robert has been working with his daughter Susan Entsminger and Pinyon Publishing to preserve and digitize these fragile glass plates (see page 139) and to share the beautiful images.

When Robert received the glass plates, most were still housed in the original sleeves labeled by Harold Taylor. The image captions in this book are based on the information from those sleeves. If necessary, supplementary information was added. The image reference numbers in the captions also come from the original sleeves and identify the images in the physical and digital archives. Glass plate negatives, though fragile and heavy, permit stunning clarity and depth of light—and celluloid would all but replace them by the late 1920s.

Vintage Yosemite displays Taylor's sensibility to Yosemite's grand views. We watch light move through giant sequoias, across rock faces, and along rivers, streams, lakes, and waterfalls. Together with visitors, wagons, and cabins of the era, we experience Yosemite as it was over one hundred years ago. *Vintage Yosemite* reveals subtleties of transformation and rhythms of magnificence.

HAROLD A. TAYLOR IN YOSEMITE

> "Being young I used to walk all the trails and carry my photographic outfit which in those days was no small item, 8 x 10 camera, tripod, and glass plates, but I thought nothing of it and often would outwalk the mules."
> —Harold A. Taylor

In the winter of 1902-3, Harold Taylor and Eugene Hallett formed the Studio of the Three Arrows in Yosemite Valley, named for Taylor's family crest and the Yosemite Miwok Indians. Their studio was accompanied by four others: George Fiske, described by Taylor: "the pioneer was a grand old gentleman and his collection of photographs especially snow scenes were superb, I doubt if they have ever been surpassed"; Julius Boysen, who Taylor worked for in the summer of 1902; Daniel J. Foley; and Harry Best, Ansel Adams' father-in-law. Ansel Adams himself was born in 1902 and would first visit the park about a decade after Taylor finished his tenure there. Taylor's time in Yosemite coincides with the success of John Muir's campaigns with President Theodore Roosevelt to bring Yosemite under the protection of the federal government.

In the first decade of the 20th century, Yosemite was still quite primitive but growing fast. Taylor loved to hear Galen Clark, the "first guardian of the valley," tell of the "early" days.

Of Mr. Curry (of Camp Curry, which "for $2.00 a day ... would provide guests with a tent, good food and the company of like-minded souls"), Taylor recalled his "stentorious voice ... calling to Glacier Point every evening."

From 1902-1907, the fee to operate his studio in Yosemite rose from $1/year to $250/year.

Regarding access into Yosemite Valley, Taylor said: "We did not spend the winters in the valley, usually coming in April every year[,] and the Yosemite Valley railroad was not built. This necessitated our getting our supplies in late in the fall for the next spring, as the roads were not opened for freight travel until May often. Six horse teams used to bring it from Raymond via Wawona."

Taylor remembers the first electricity in Yosemite: "The first summer I was in the valley they built the electric light plant at Happy Isles and I remember well when the first lights were turned on."

In 1907, Taylor and Hallett sold the Studio of the Three Arrows to Arthur C. Pillsbury.

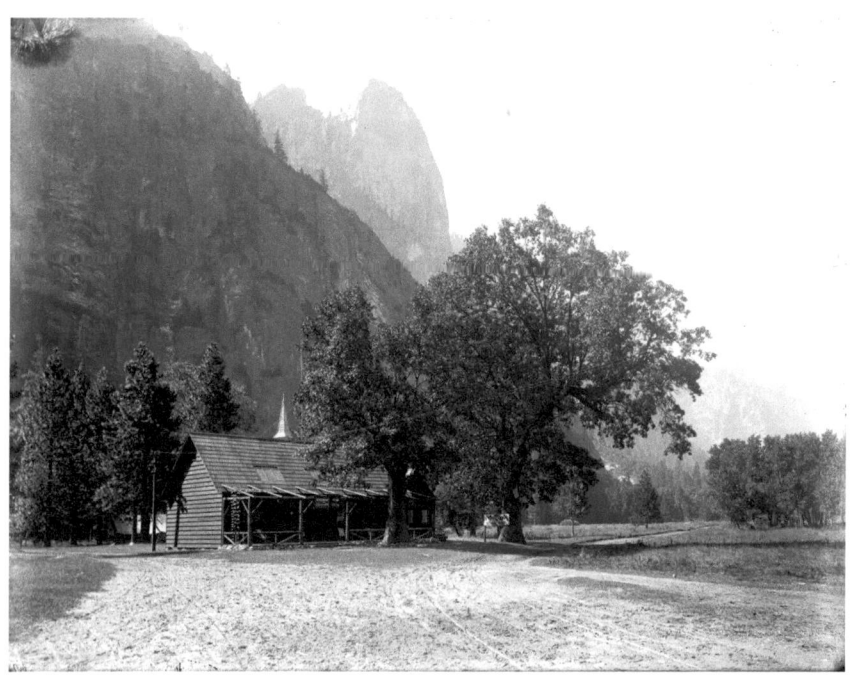

Studio of the Three Arrows (672, 6.5" x 8.5")
Chapel and Sentinel Rock in background.

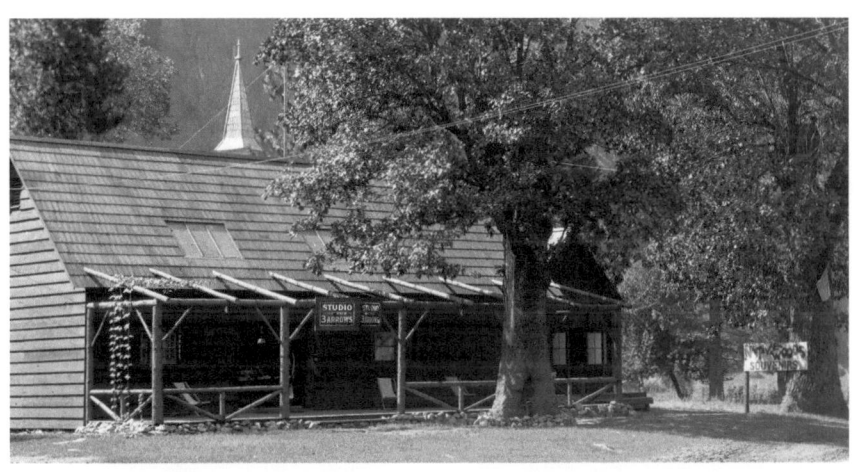

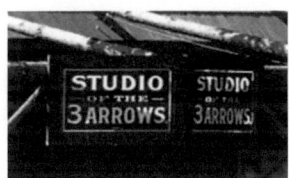 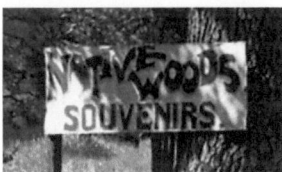

Detail of *Studio of the Three Arrows* (672, 6.5" x 8.5")

Valley Views

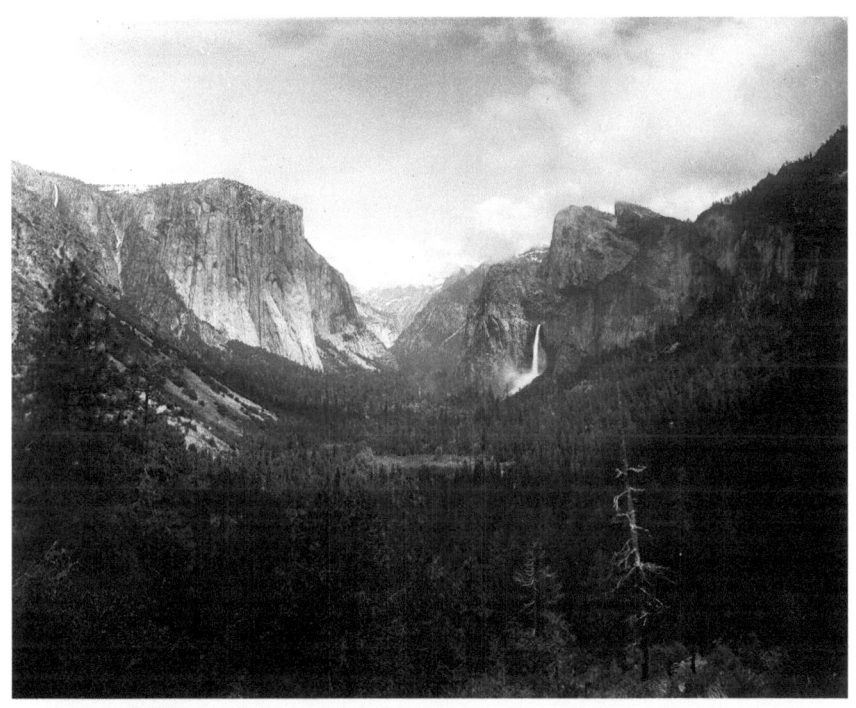

Entrance to Yosemite, View from Historic Artist Point (627a, 8" x 10")

Today (in the 21st century) when one enters Yosemite National Park from the South Entrance at Wawona, the first spectacular view of Yosemite Valley is a vista now called Tunnel View.

After driving 25 miles through pine and oak forests you pass through the Wawona Tunnel—about four-fifths of a mile blasted through granite, completed in 1933. The road then emerges along the south rim of Yosemite Valley. The panorama includes many of the beloved features of Yosemite Valley: El Capitan, Clouds Rest, Half Dome, Sentinel Rock, Sentinel Dome, Cathedral Rocks, and Bridalveil Fall.

A hiking trail leading up from Tunnel View takes you to several other awe-inspiring vistas, some of which are named: Artist, Inspiration, Crocker, Stanford, Dewey, Taft.

Harold Taylor took photographs in this area in the early 20th century (before the tunnel). The photographic plates that he labeled as Inspiration Point and Artist Point may not contain the exact vistas that we connect with those names today. While they were undoubtedly taken in the vicinity of what we now know as Tunnel View, what he noted as "Artist Point" looks more like what we now know as "Inspiration Point" and vice versa. The collection of vistas in the vicinity of Tunnel View vary in whether certain features are visible or not (e.g., Sentinel Dome, Royal Arches, and North Dome).

To investigate the precise location of Artist Point, we go back 50 years before Taylor's photographs to the first recorded drawing of Yosemite, a pencil drawing made by Thomas Ayres in 1855. The vista in Ayres' famous "Artist Point" drawing doesn't look precisely like what we now know as Artist Point; but it looks more like Taylor's "Artist Point." So perhaps Taylor and Ayres's Artist Point might be

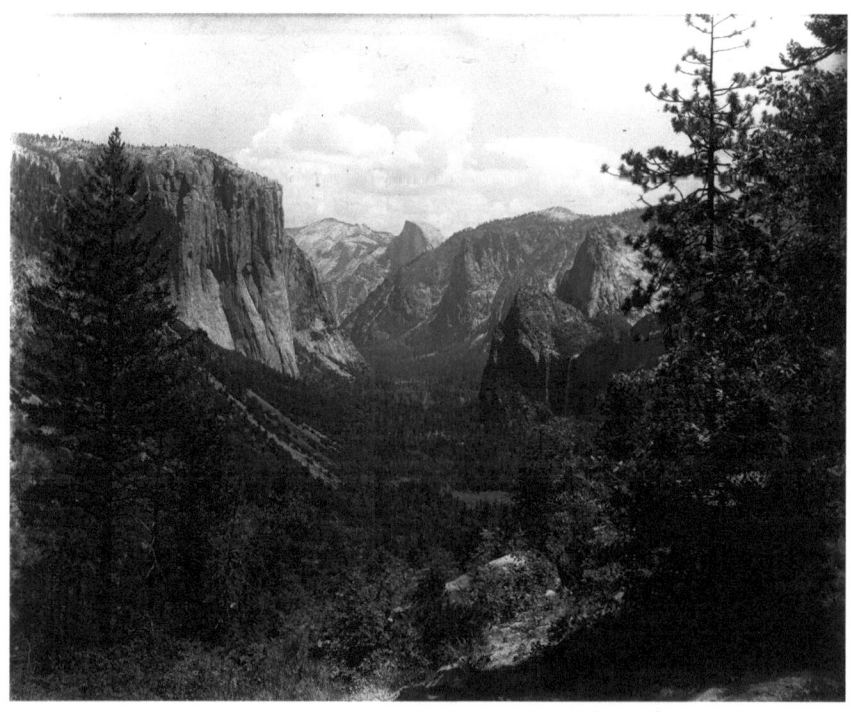

View from Historic Inspiration Point (537, 8" x 10")

thought of as the "Historic" or "Original" Artist Point. Similarly, Taylor's Inspiration Point, looks like George Fiske's late 19th-century photograph of Inspiration point, now called "Old Inspiration Point."

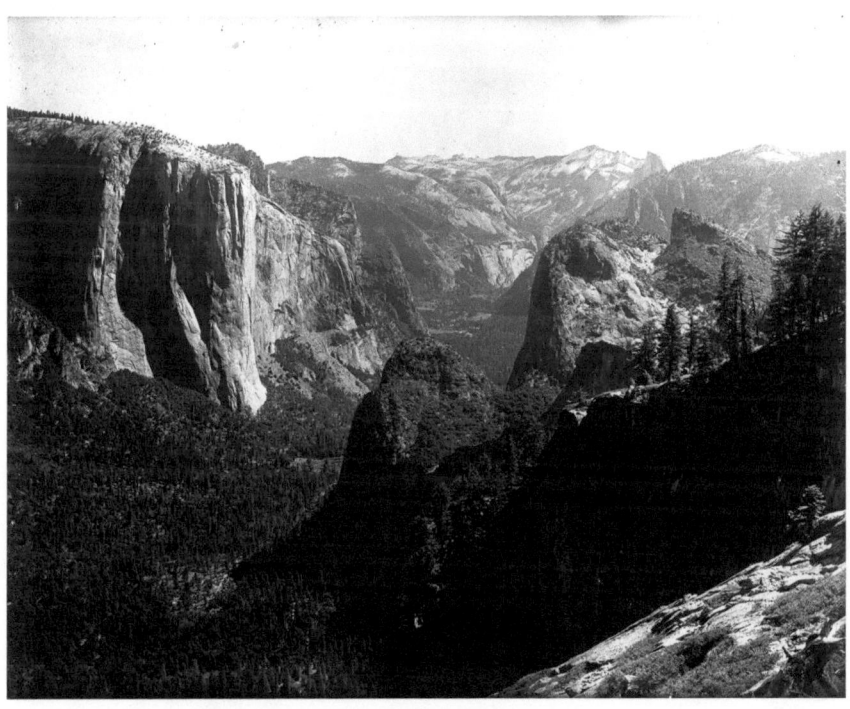

View from Stanford Point (542, 6.5" x 8.5")

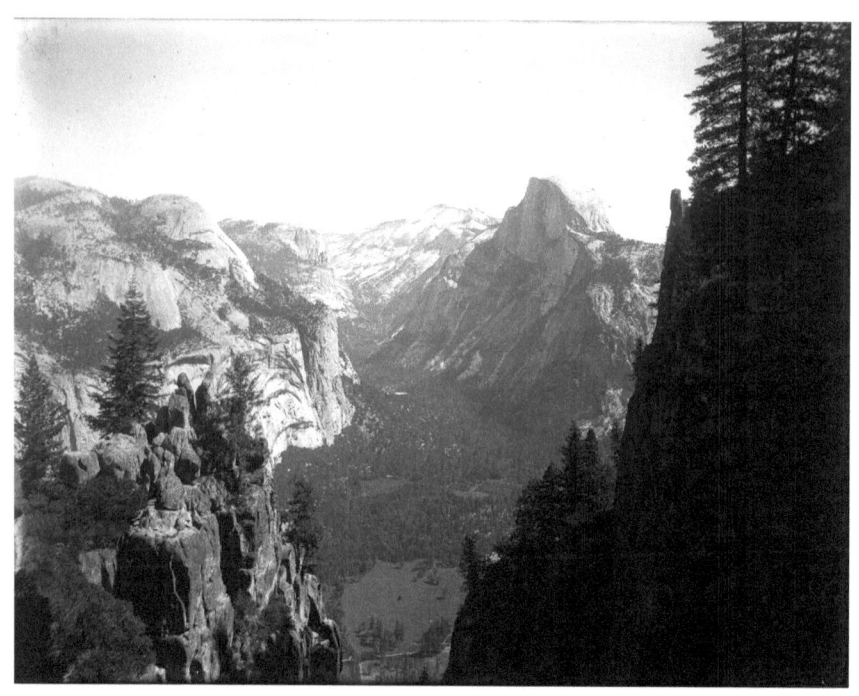

View from Moran Point (600, 6.5" x 8.5")

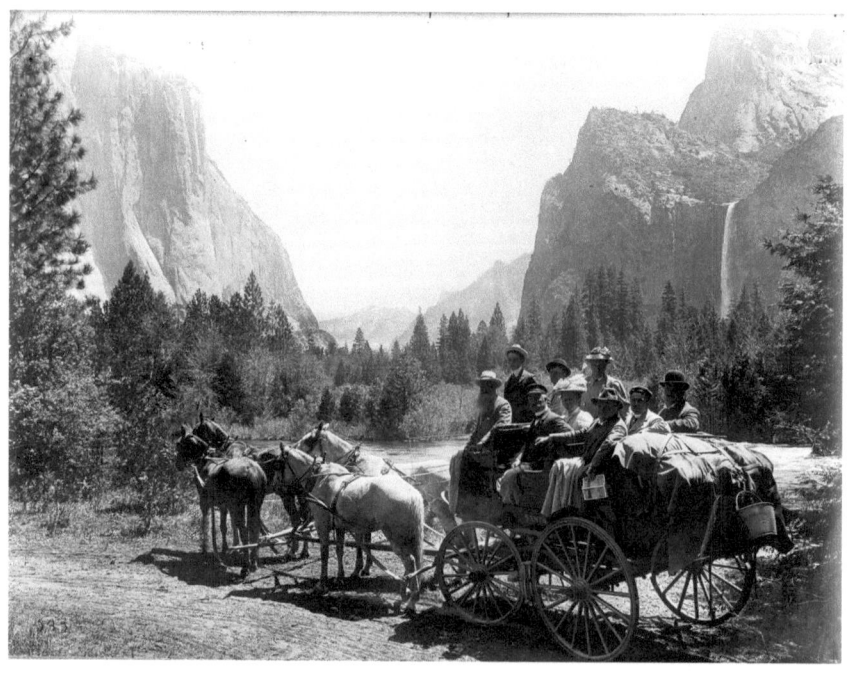

Gates of the Valley, with 9 People in Wagon, 4 horses (679b, 6.5" x 8.5")

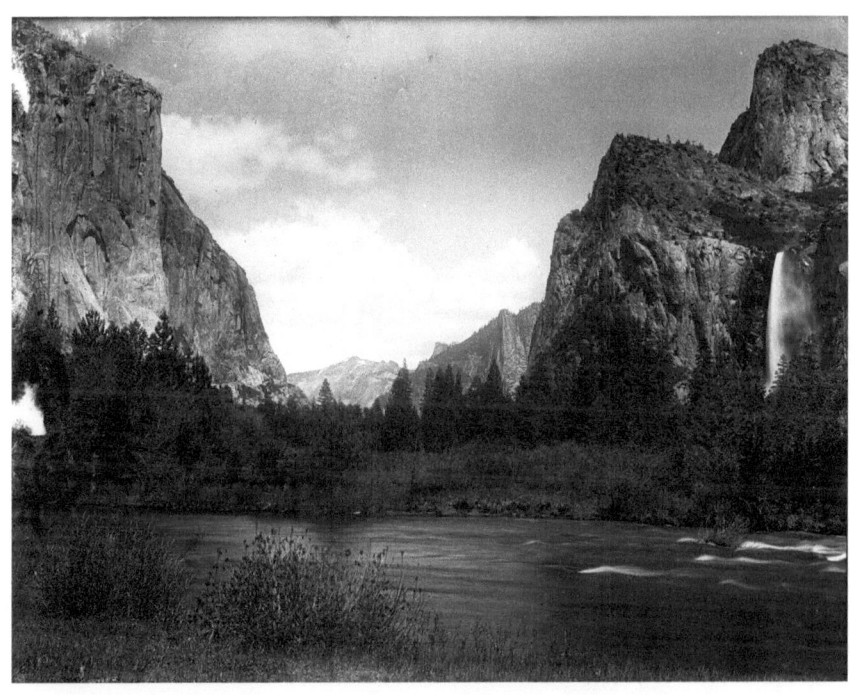

Gates of the Valley with Merced River and Bridalveil Fall (558a, 6.5" x 8.5")

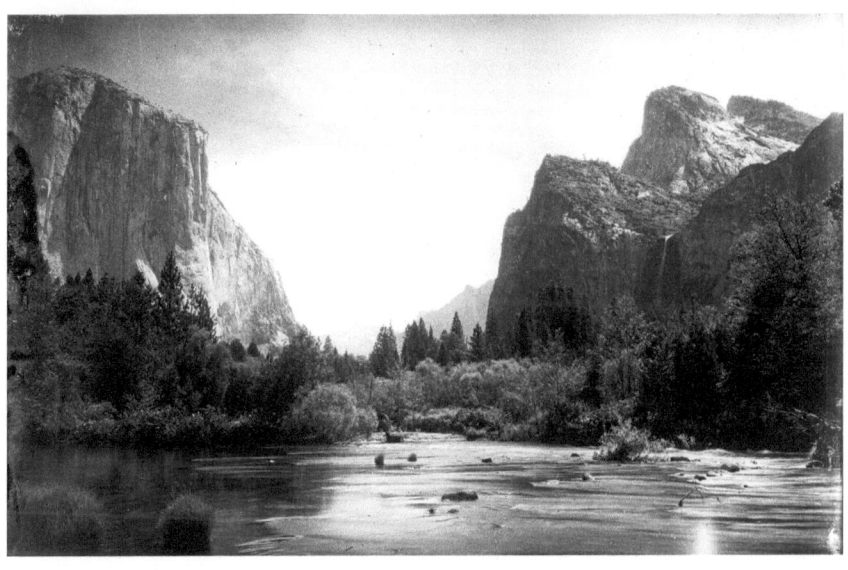

Gates of the Valley with Merced River and Bridalveil Fall (558b, 6.5" x 8.5")

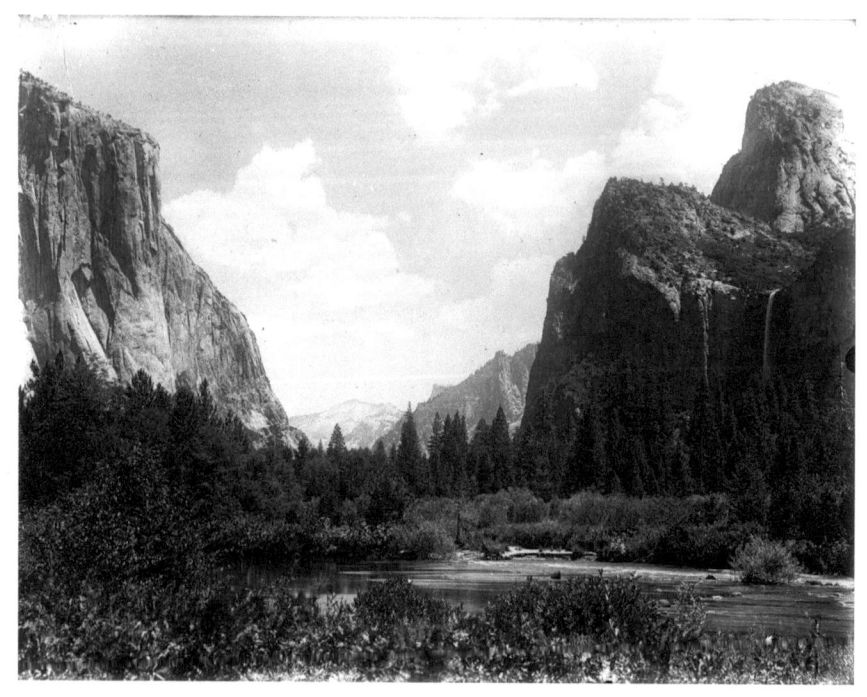

Gates of the Valley: July 24, 1903 (562, 6.5" x 8.5")

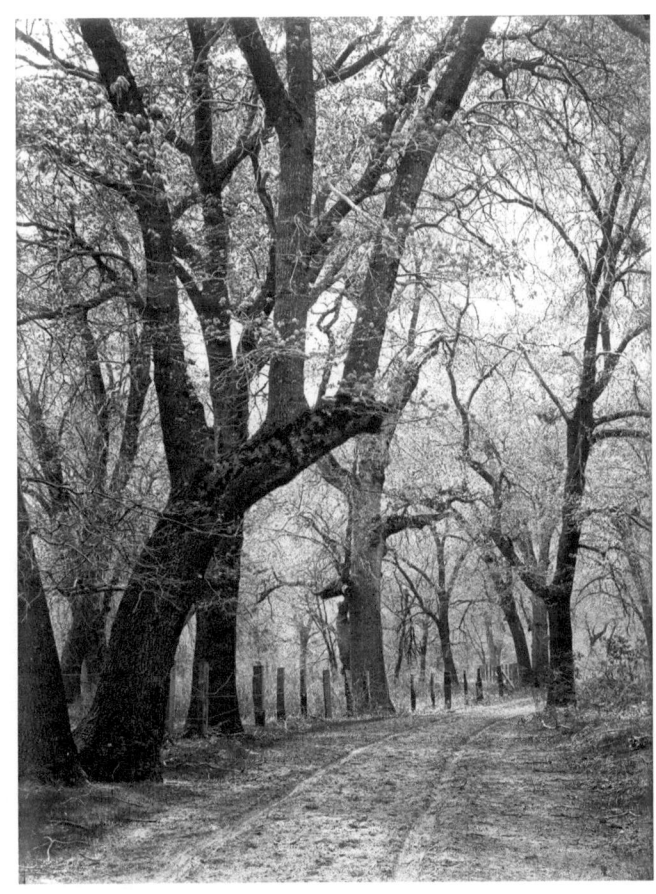

Oak Trees, Yosemite Valley (615, 6.5" x 8.5")

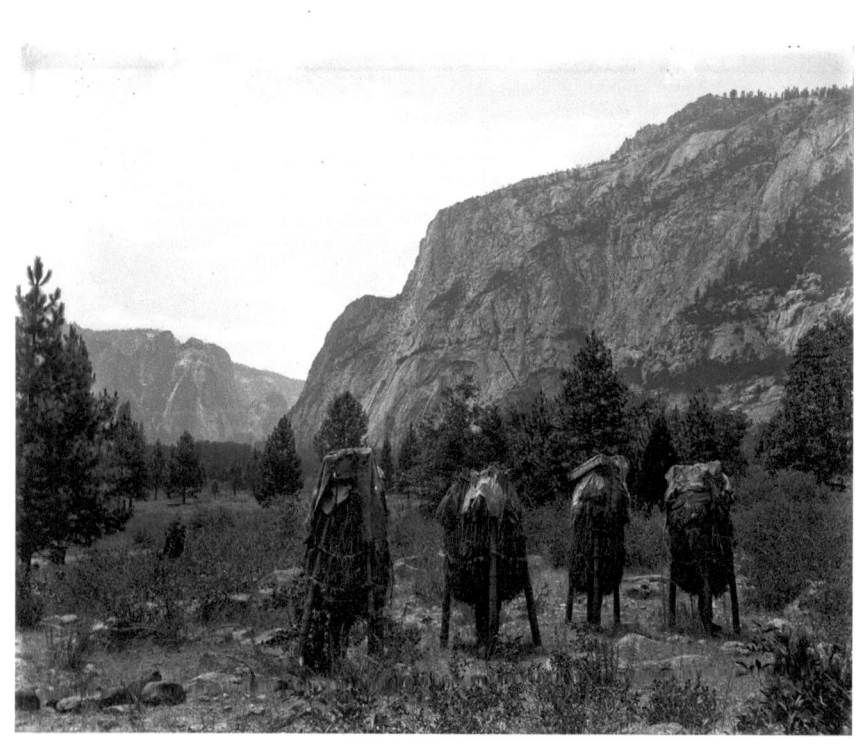

Indian Acorn Cache (531, 8" x 10")

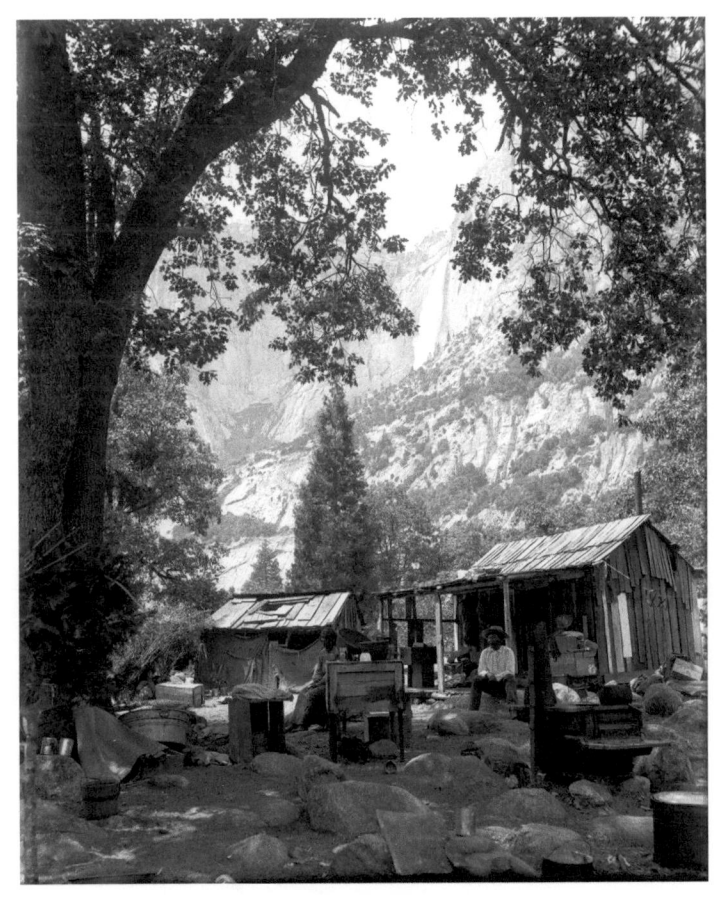

Indian Camp (528, 8" x 10")

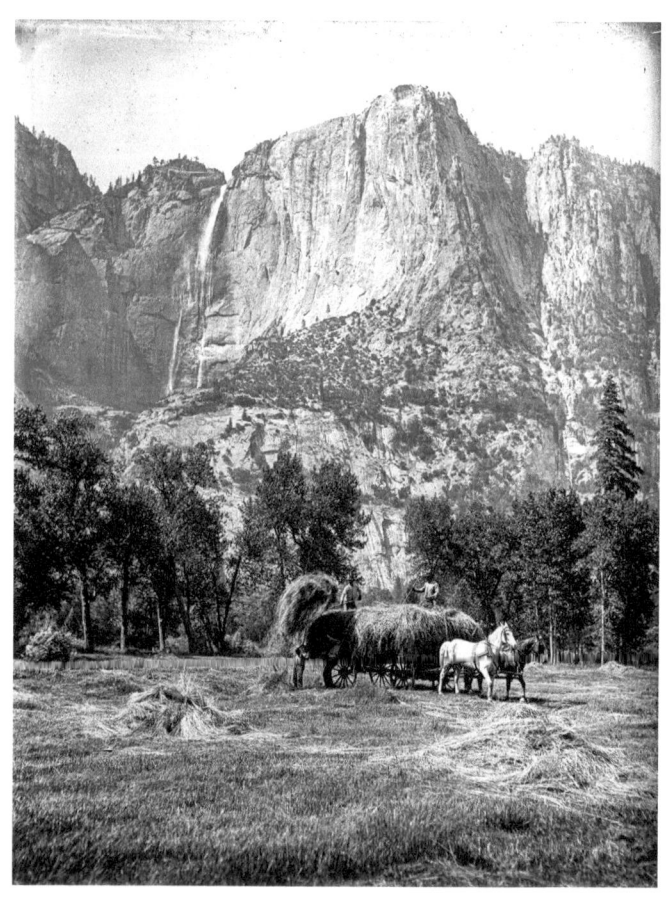

Haymaking Wagon below Yosemite Falls in Cook's Meadow (503a, 8" x 10")

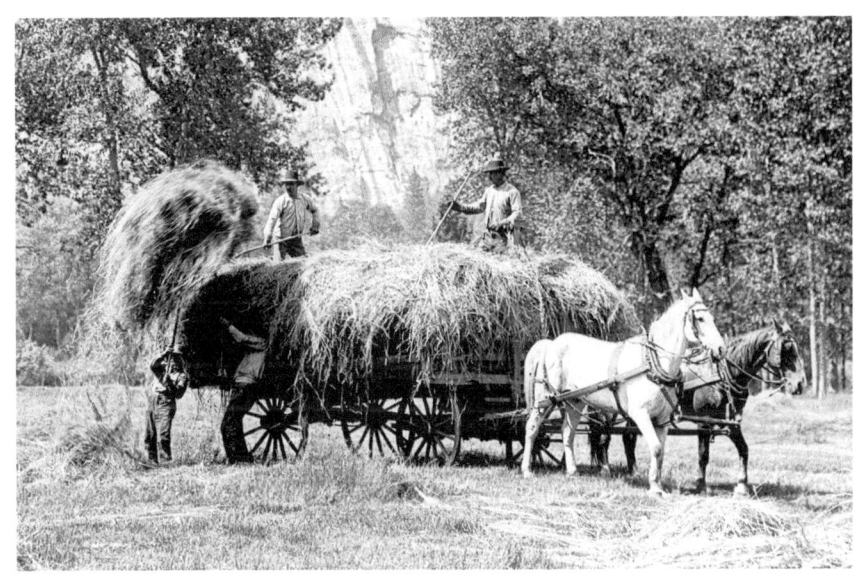

Detail of *Haymaking Wagon* (503a, 8" x 10")

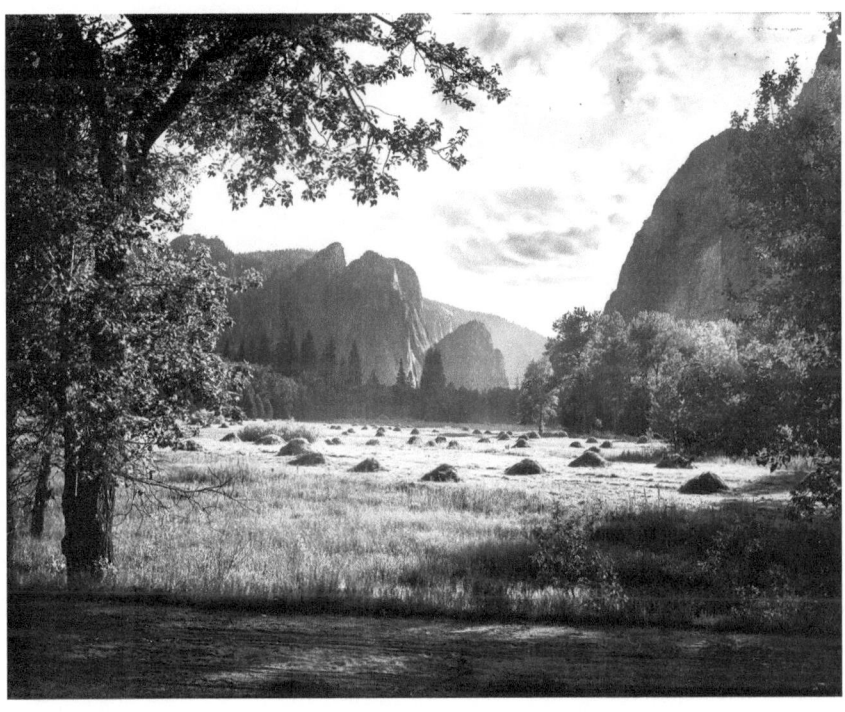

Haying Piles Leidig Meadow, Looking West toward Cathedral Rocks (674a, 8" x 10")

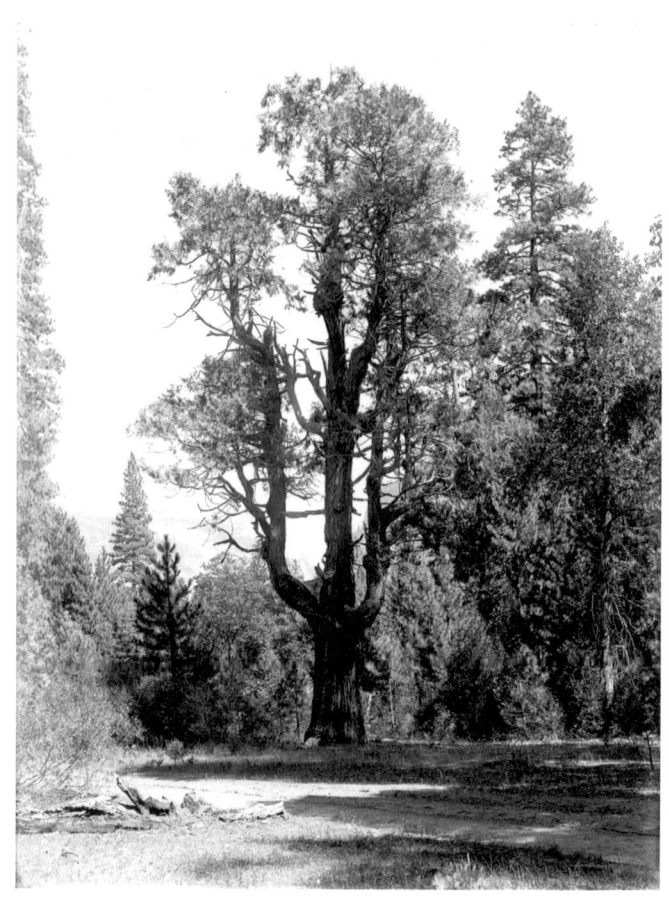

Big Cedar Tree (661, 6.5" x 8.5")
Harold Taylor subtitled this image "Harp of O[b]eron," which might reference Elias Parish Alvars's 1842 solo harp music adapted from Carl Maria Weber's 1826 "Oberon" opera.

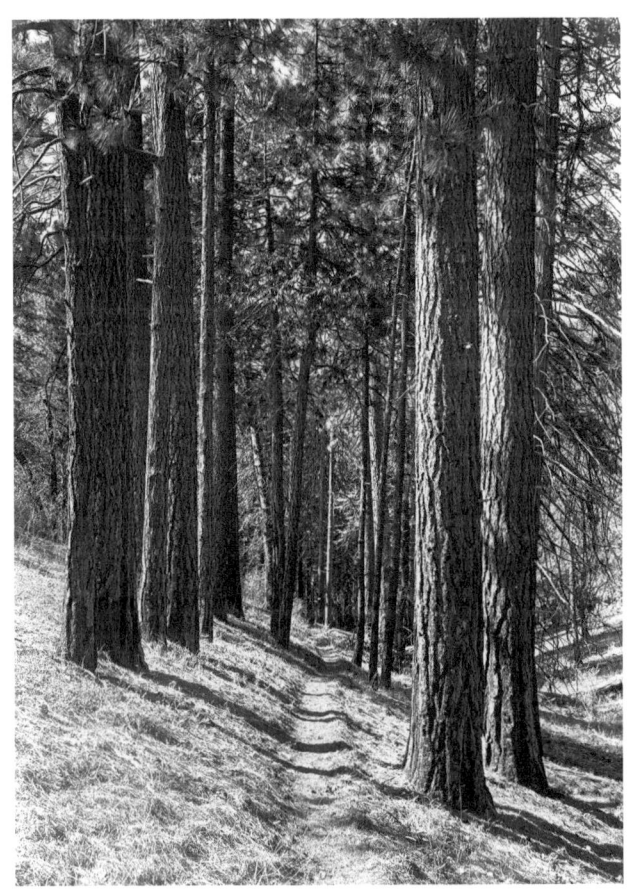

Trail through Woods (405, 5" x 7")

Waterfalls

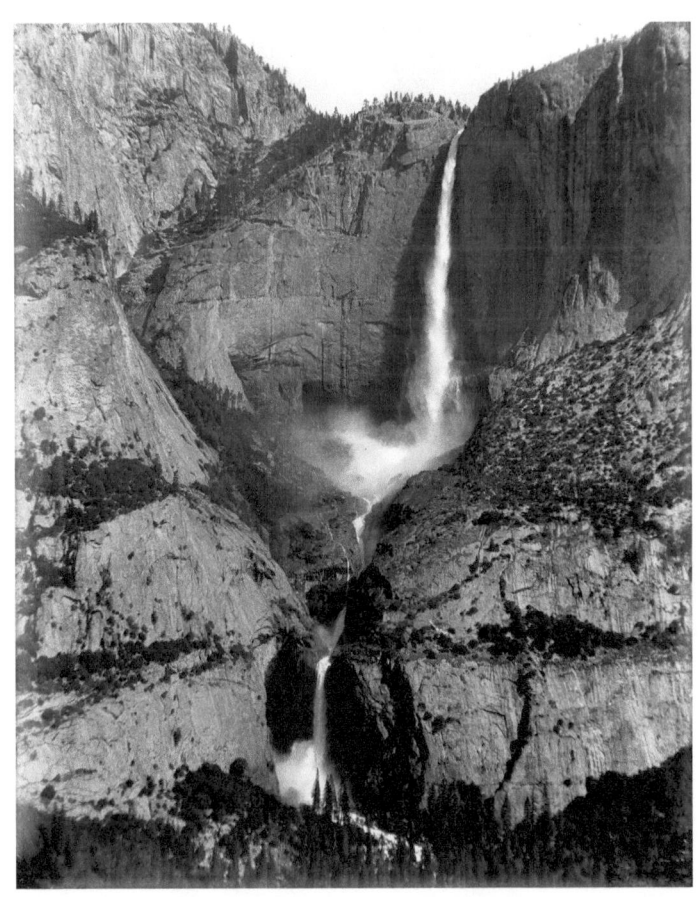

Yosemite Falls from Four Mile Trail to Glacier Point (509, 8" x 10")

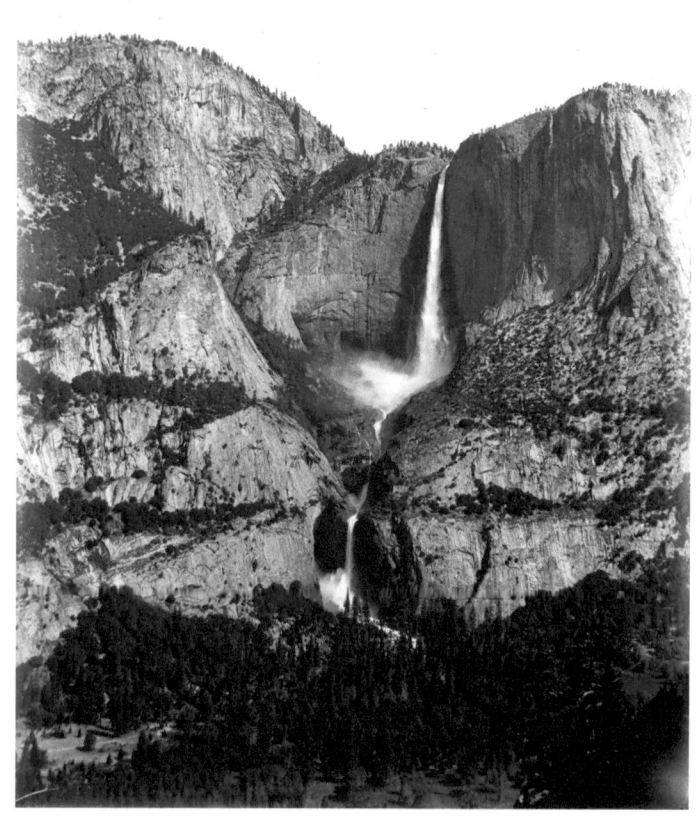

Yosemite Falls from Four Mile Trail to Glacier Point (509a, 8" x 10")

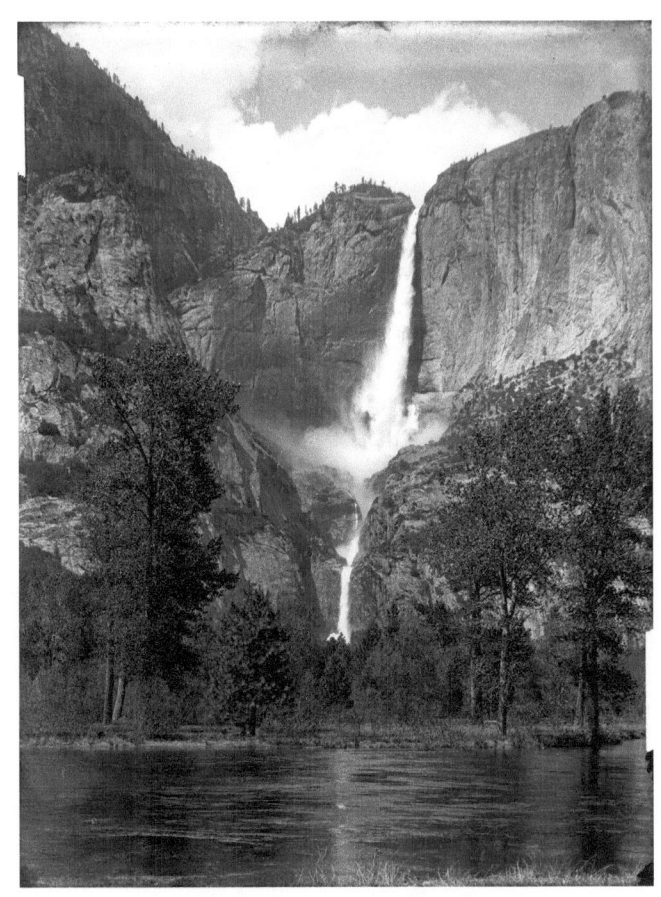
Yosemite Falls from Meadow (510, 6.5" x 8.5")

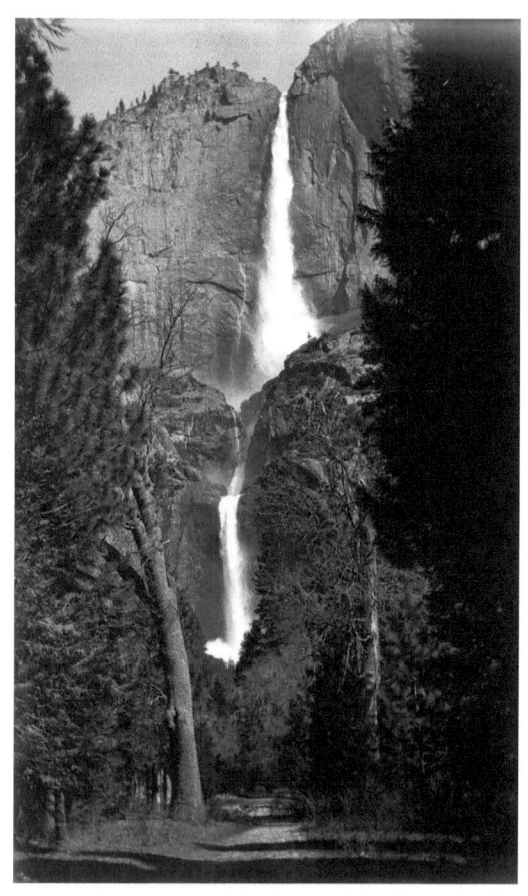

Yosemite Falls Road (Trail) (511, 6.5" x 8.5")

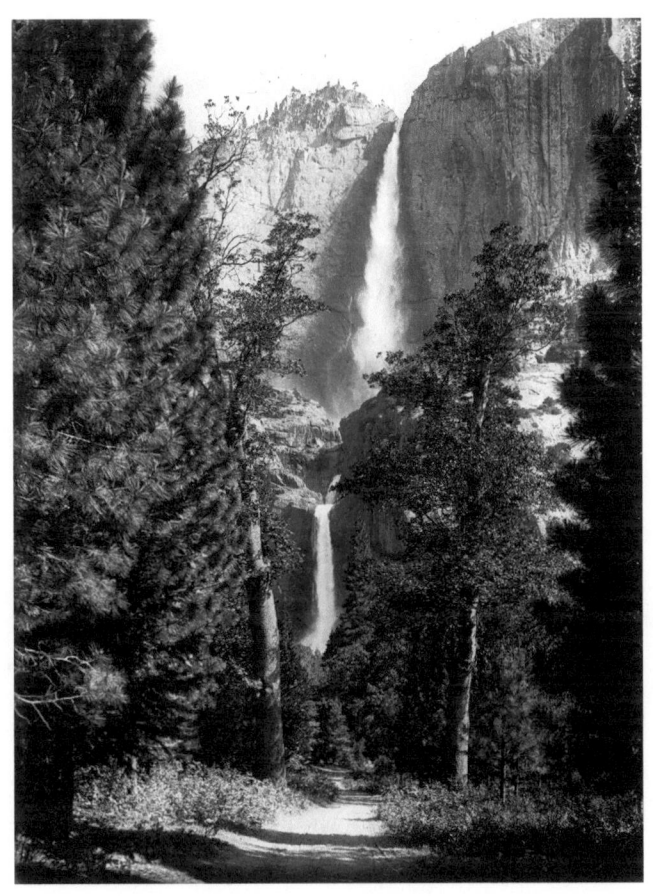

Yosemite Falls Road (Trail) (647, 6.5" x 8.5")

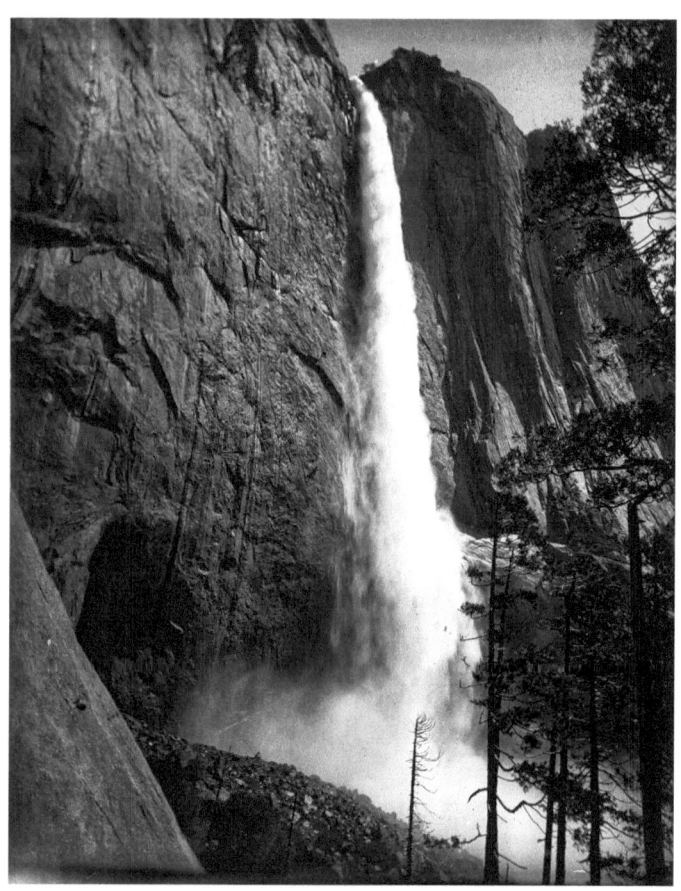

Upper Yosemite Fall (540, 8" x 10")

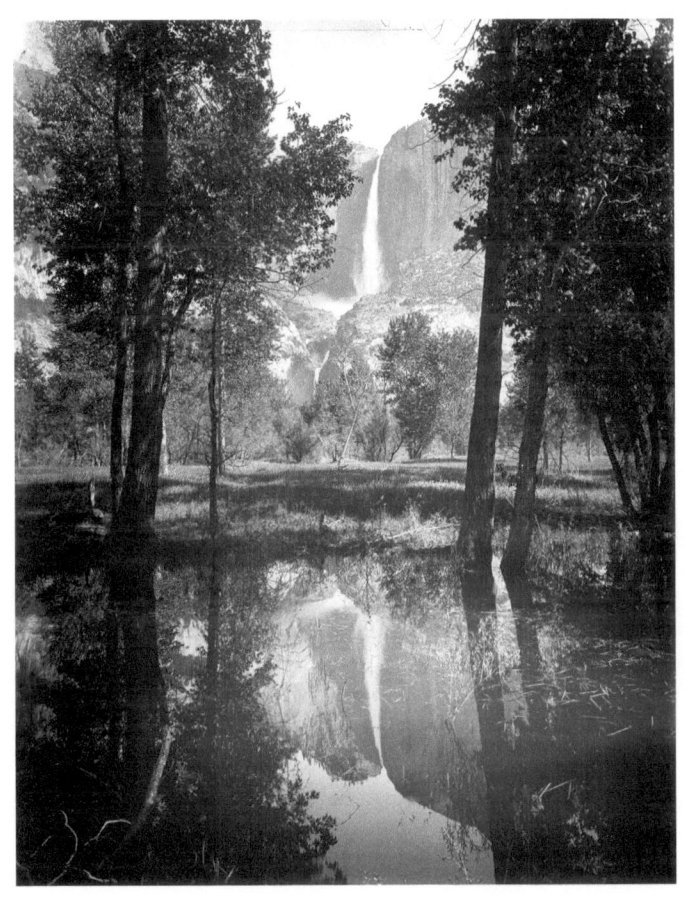

Yosemite Falls Reflection (613, 8" x 10")

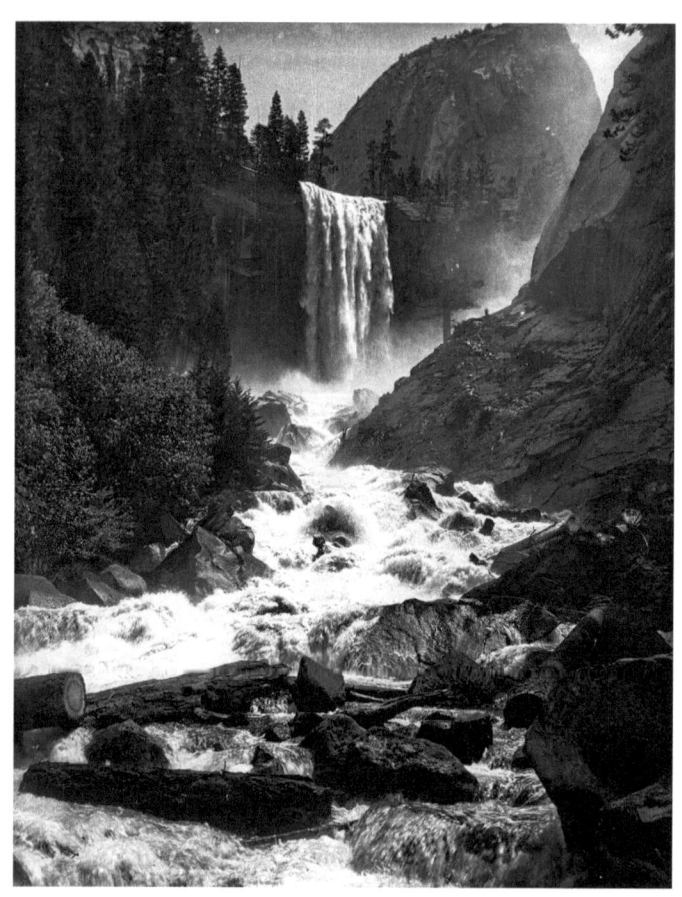

Vernal Fall (535, 8" x 10")

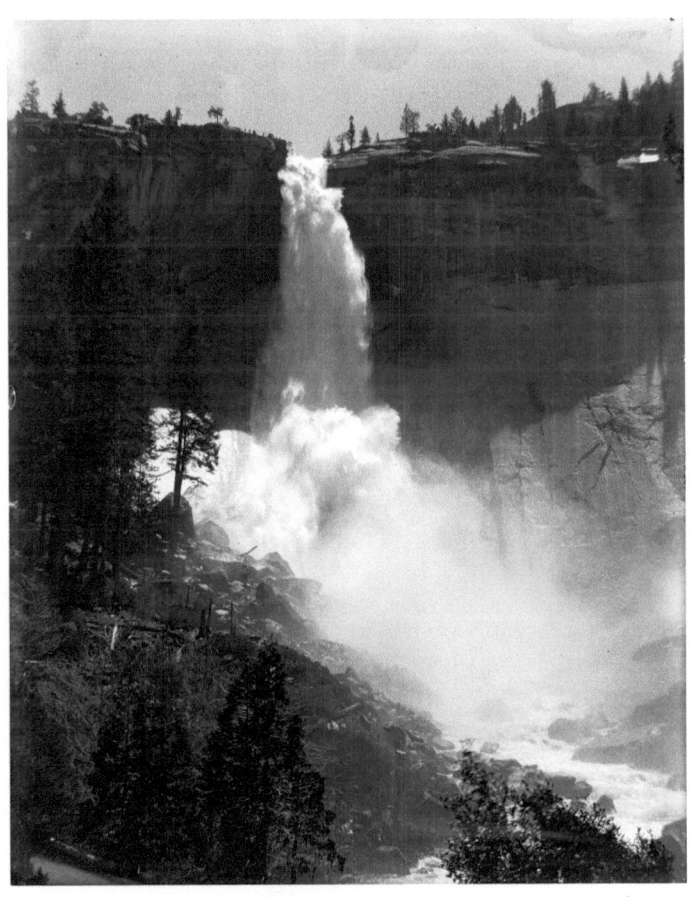

Nevada Fall (519, 8" x 10")

Harold Taylor noted that this photograph was taken from "Snows," in reference to Albert and Emily Snow's hotel, "La Casa Nevada," in operation from 1870 to 1891.

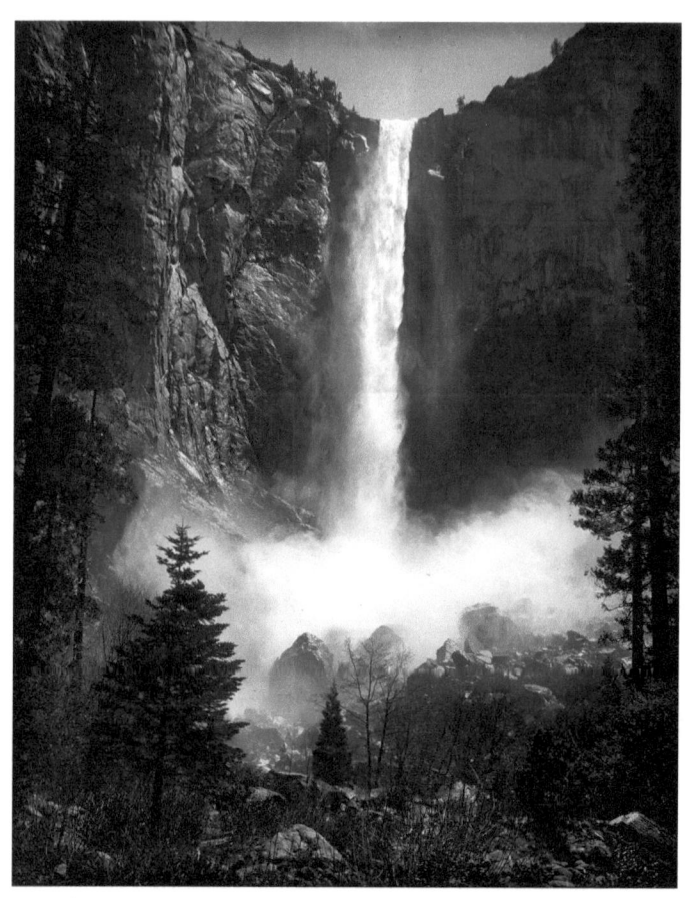

Bridalveil Fall (538, 8" x 10")

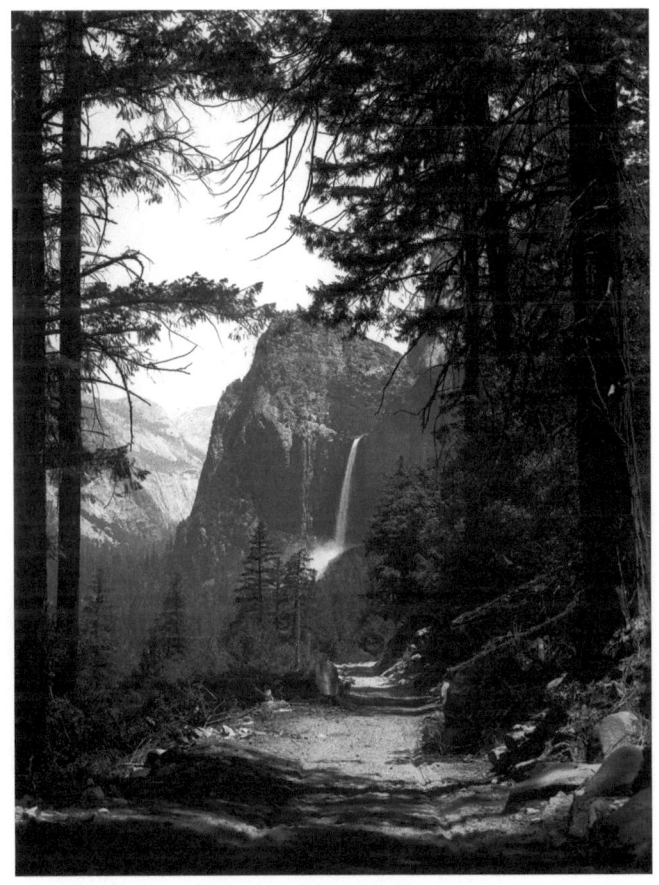

Bridalveil Fall (650, 6.5" x 8.5")
Harold Taylor noted "from Wawona Road," probably referring to the original Mariposa Road that came in from Wawona.

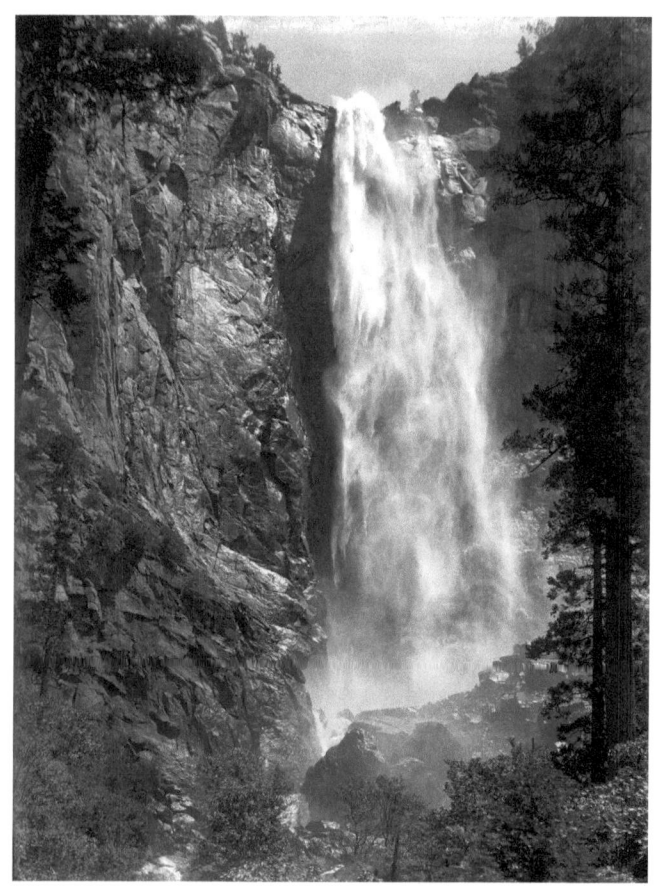

Bridalveil Fall (673, 6.5" x 8.5")

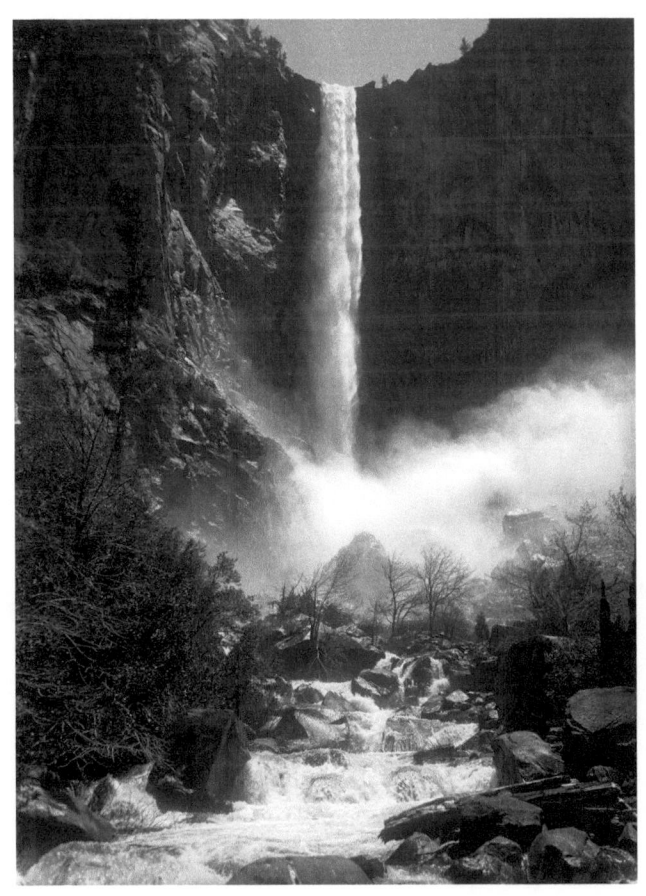

Bridalveil Fall (401, 6.5" x 8.5")

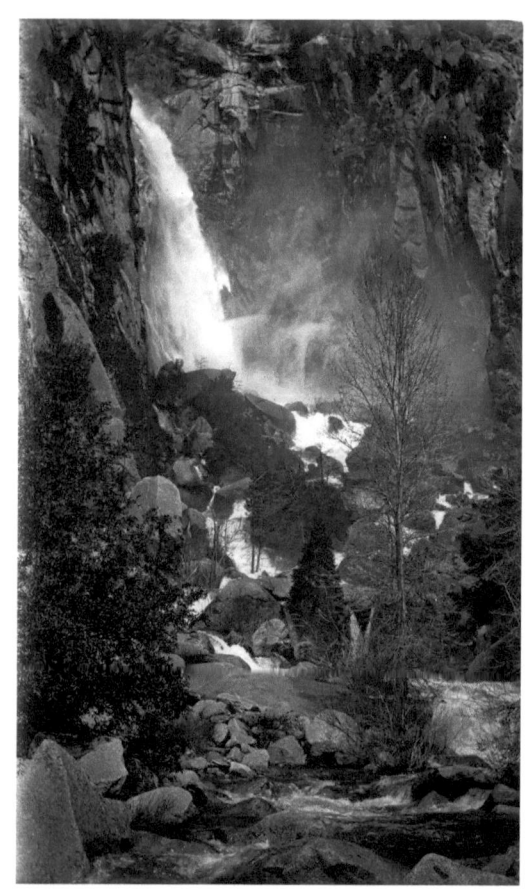

Cascade Falls (559, 6.5" x 8.5")

Rocks

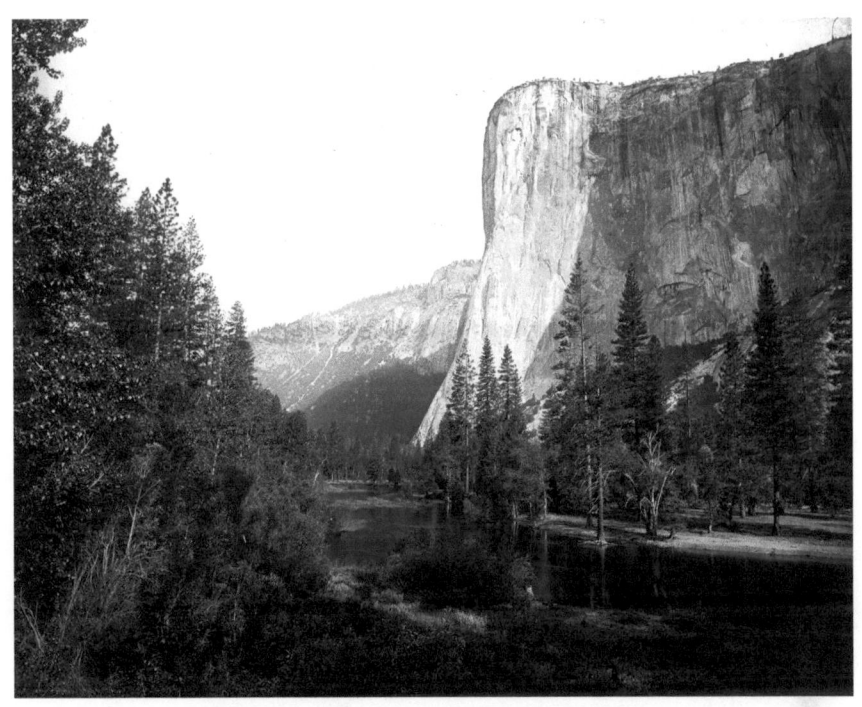

El Capitan Morning Landscape (539c, 8" x 10")

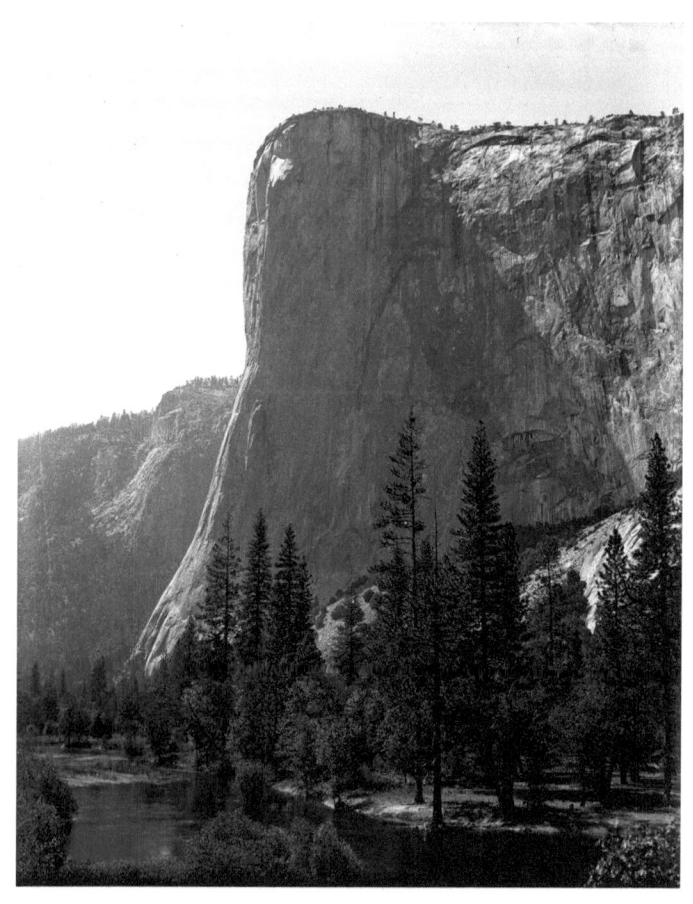

El Capitan Afternoon (586, 6.5" x 8.5")

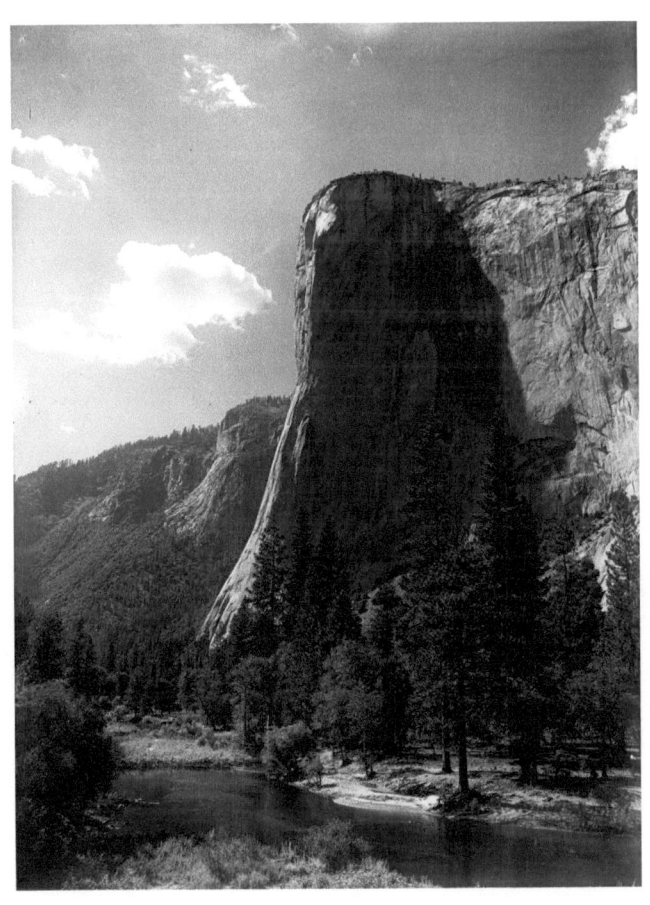

El Capitan Afternoon with Clouds (680, 6.5" x 8.5")

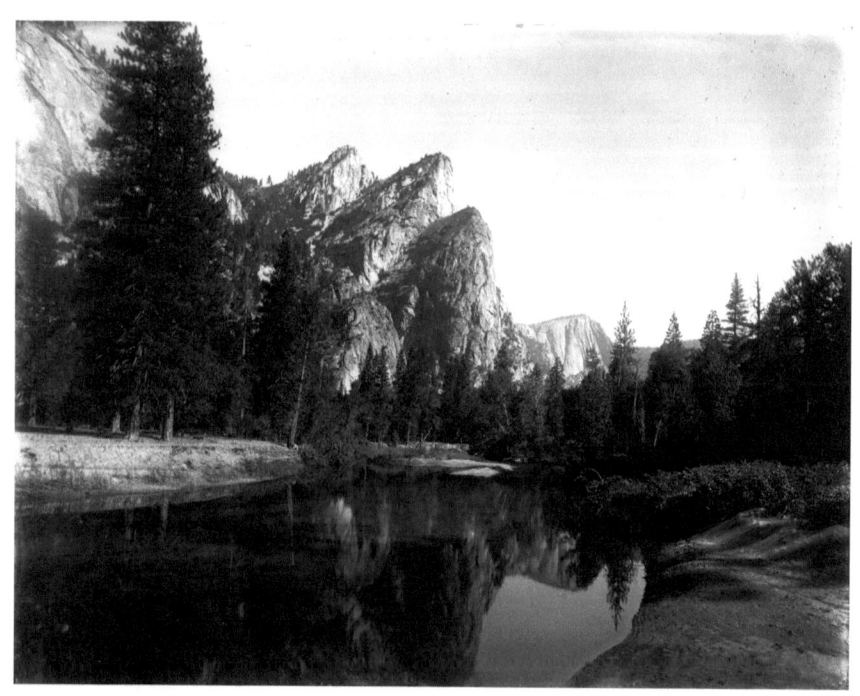

Three Brothers, Wide Angle (636, 6.5" x 8.5")

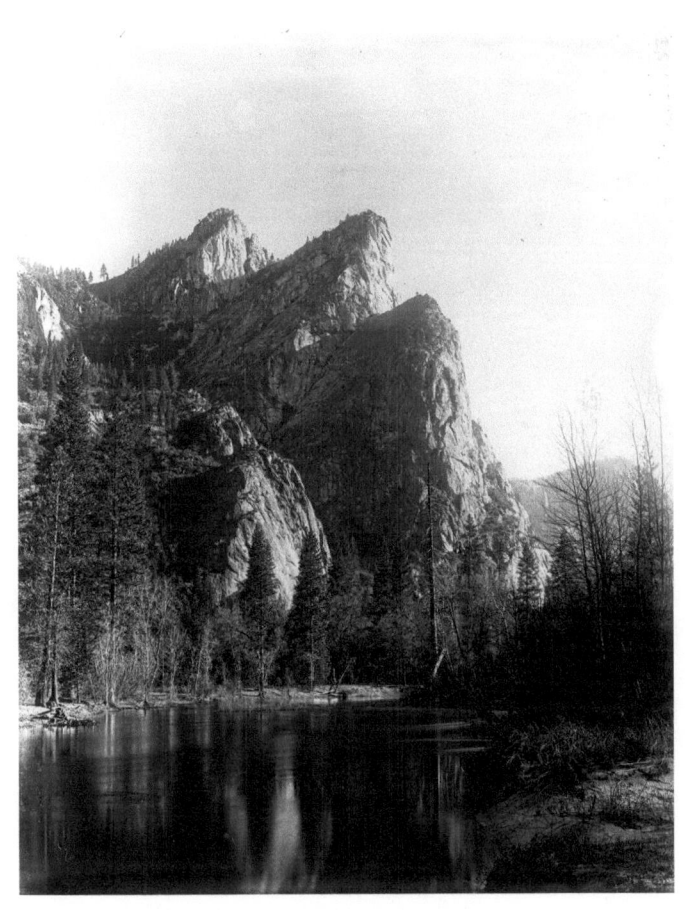

Three Brothers (534b, 8" x 10")

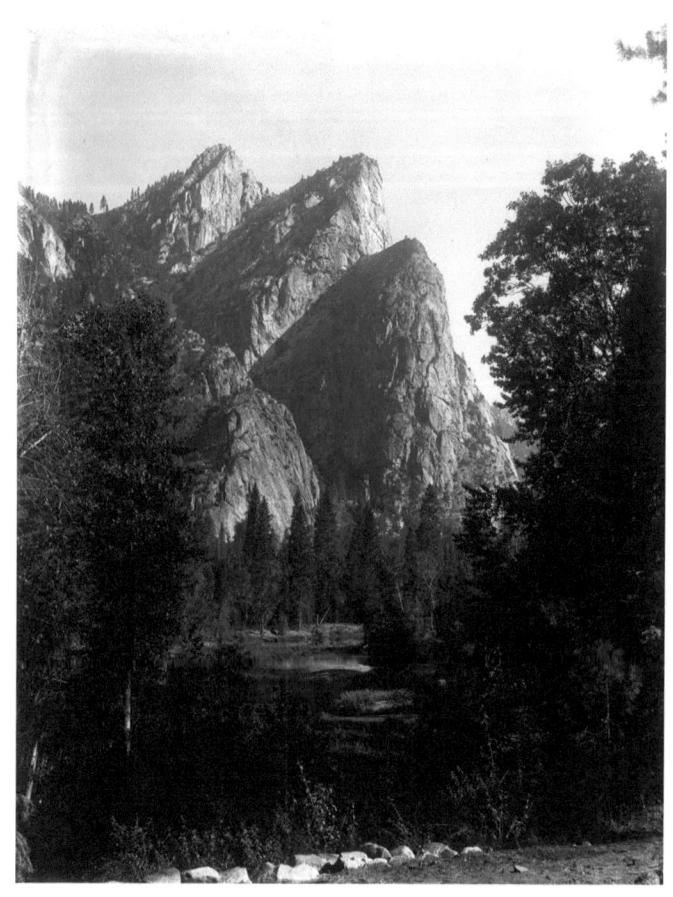

Three Brothers from the Road (583, 6.5" x 8.5")

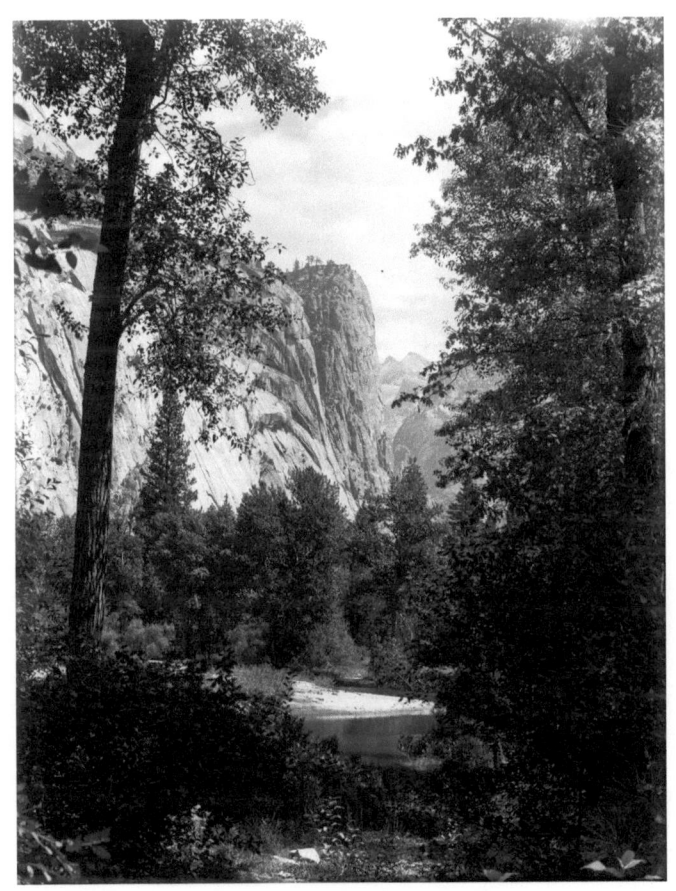

Washington Column (602, 6.5" x 8.5")

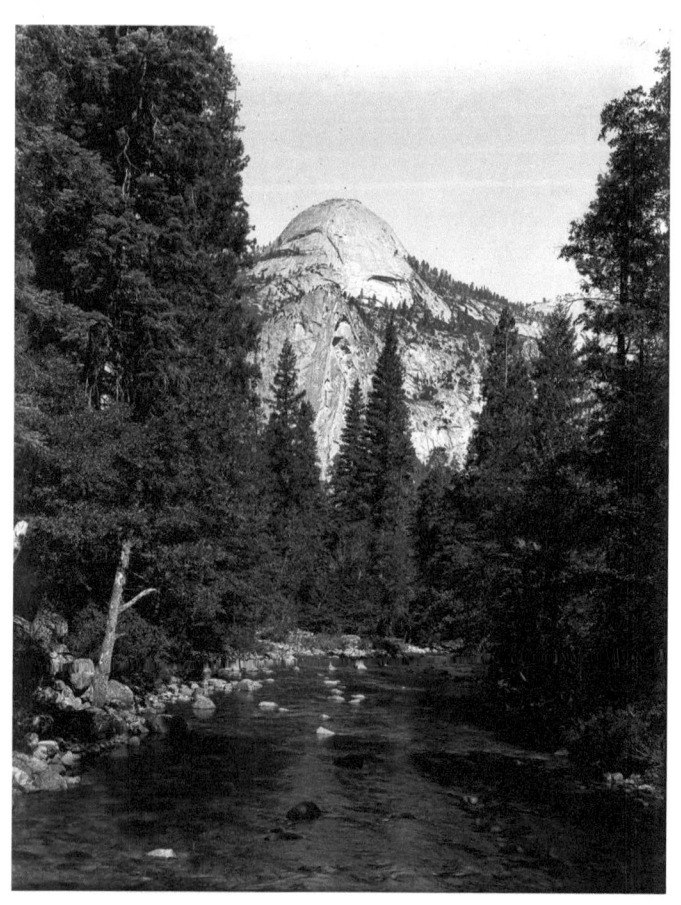

North Dome from Happy Isles (597, 6.5" x 8.5")

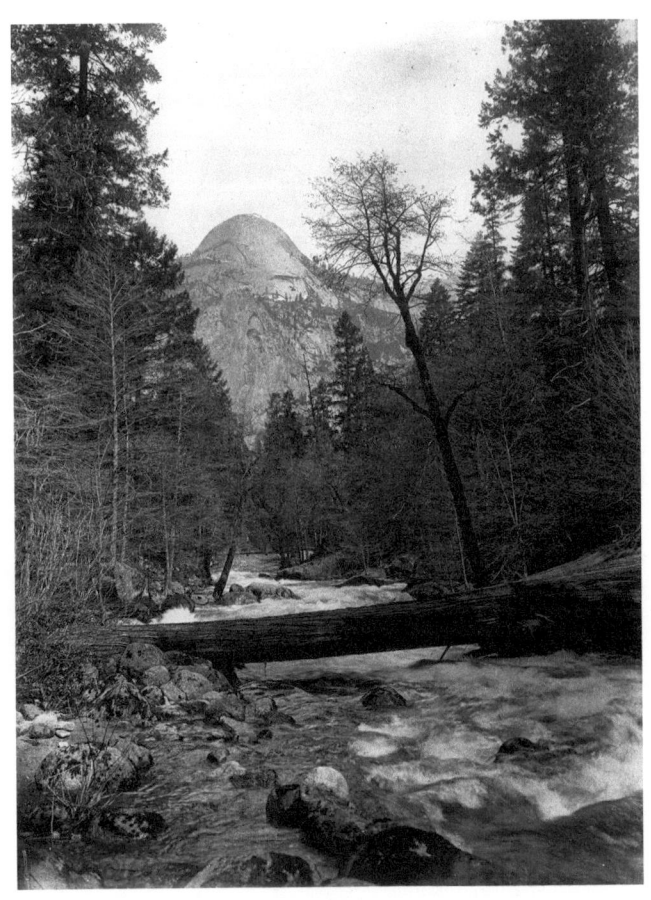

North Dome from Happy Isles (637, 6.5" x 8.5")

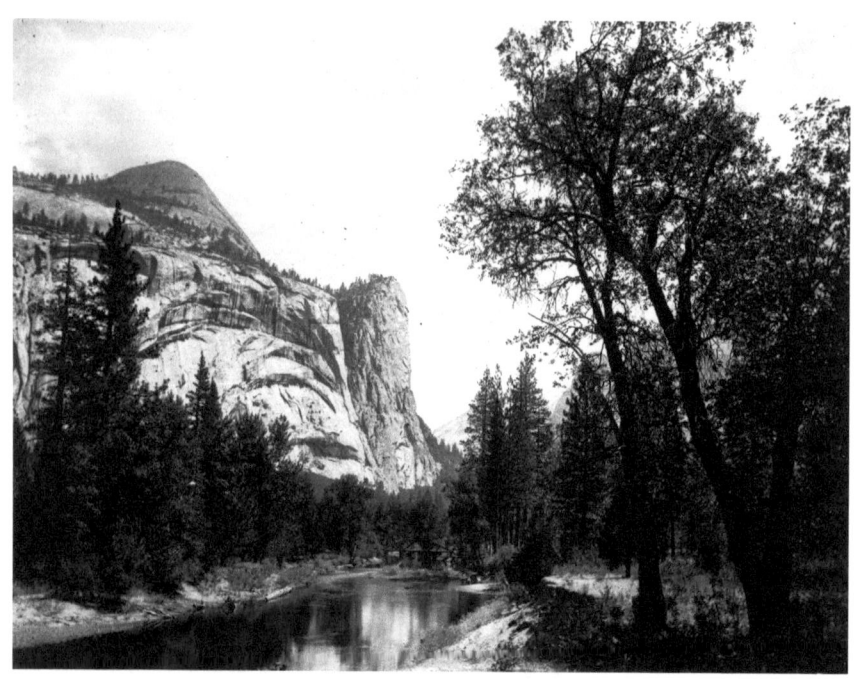

North Dome, Royal Arches, and Washington Column (677a, 6.5" x 8.5")

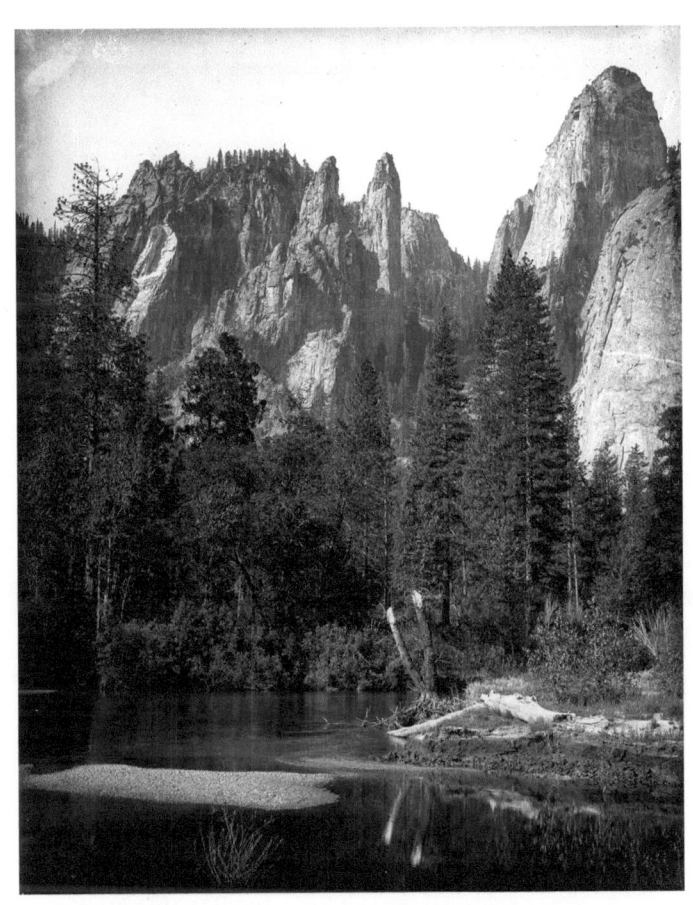

Cathedral Spires from River (536b, 8" x 10")

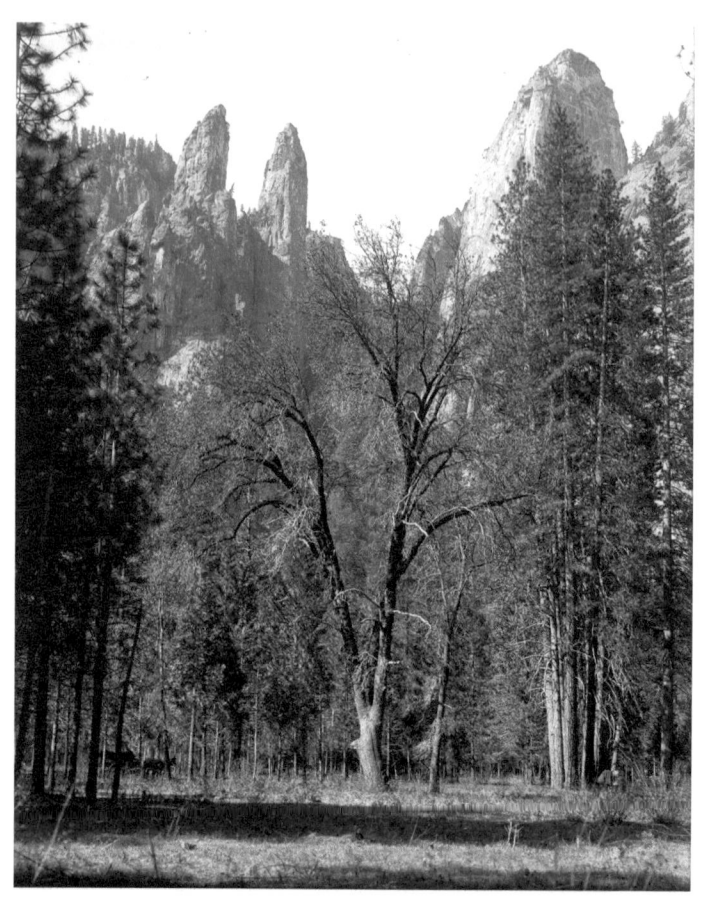

Cathedral Spires with Road and Wagon (504, 8" x 10")

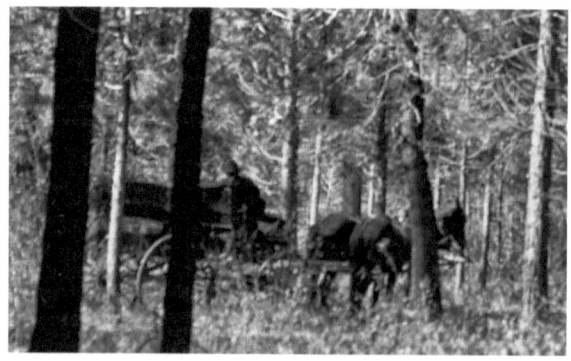

Detail of *Cathedral Spires with Road and Wagon* (504, 8" x 10")

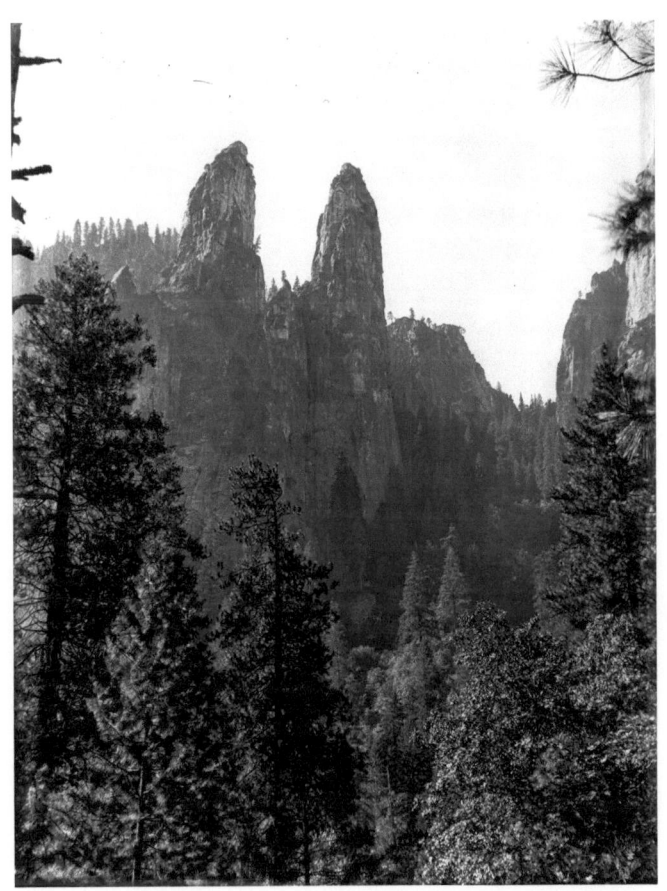
Cathedral Spires Telephoto (658, 6.5" x 8.5")

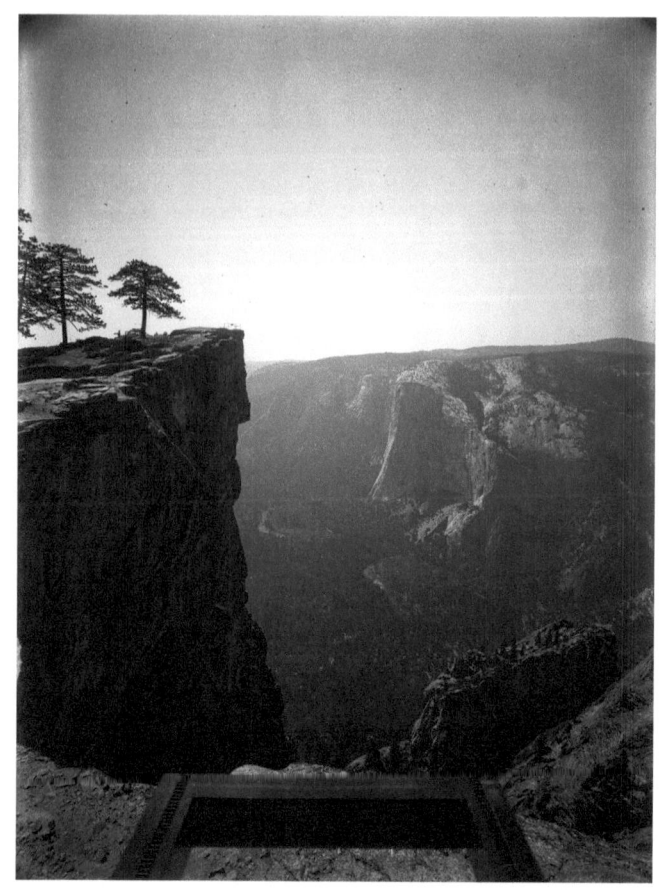

Taft Point (404, 6.5" x 8.5")

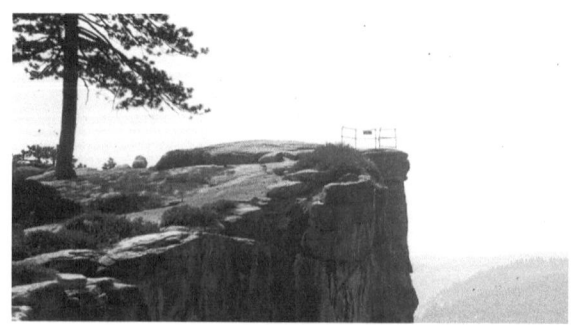

Detail of *Taft Point* (404, 6.5" x 8.5")

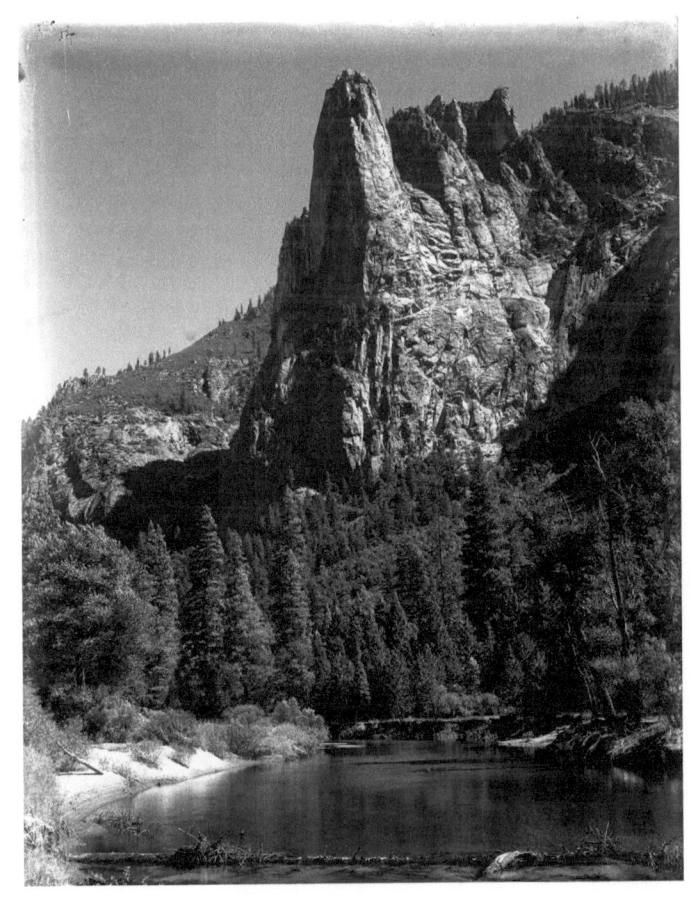

Sentinel Rock (552, 6.5" x 8.5")

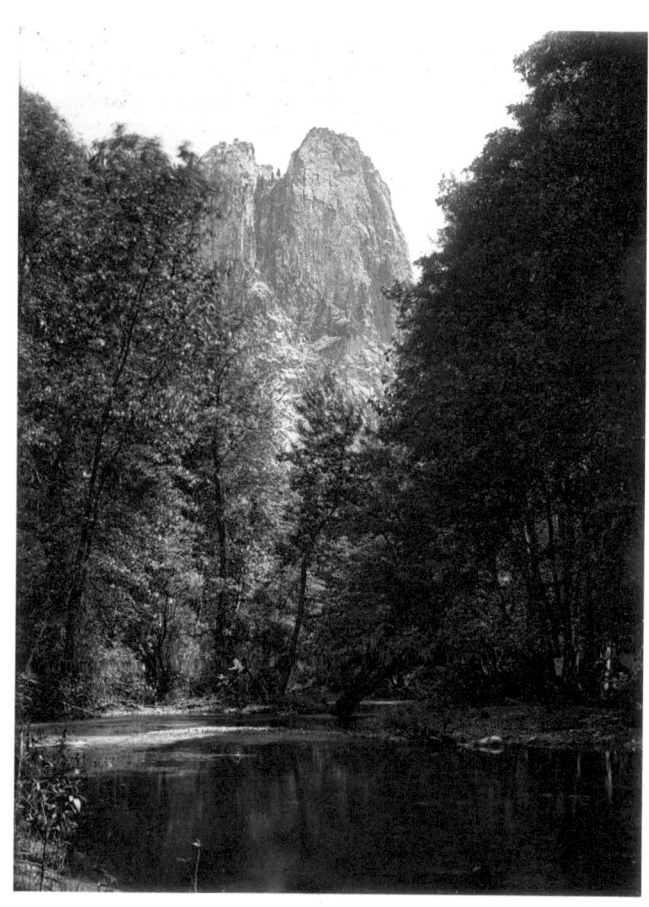

Sentinel Rock (555, 6.5" x 8.5")

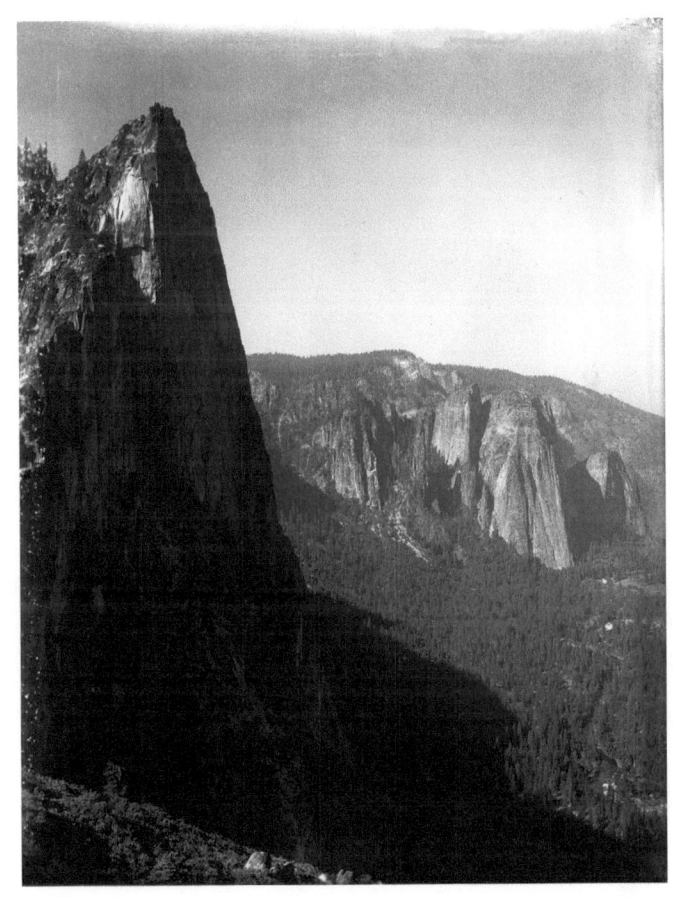

Sentinel Rock Profile with Cathedral Rocks in Background (582, 6.5" x 8.5")
View from the Four Mile Trail to Glacier Point.

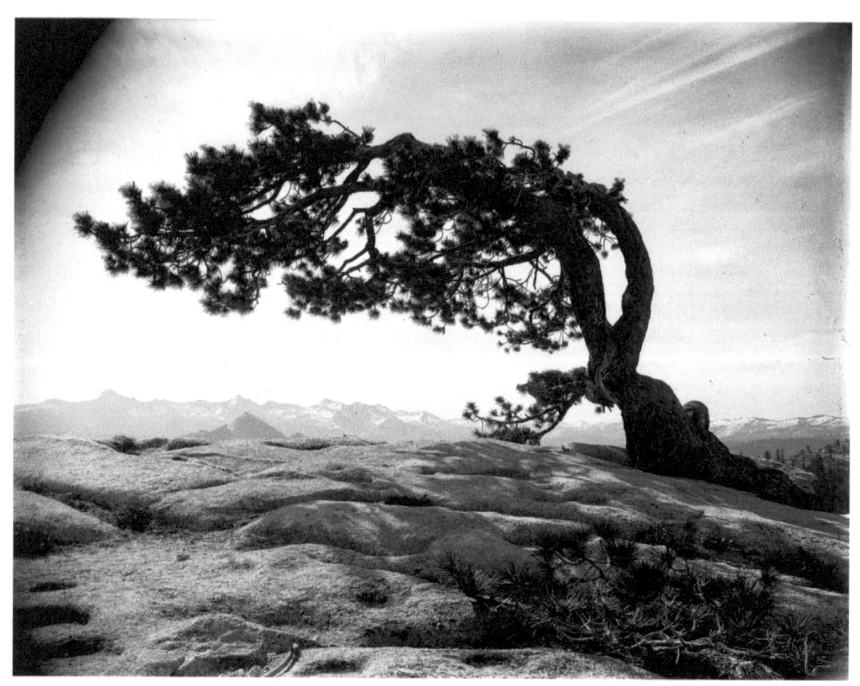

Sentinel Dome Tree (686, 6.5" x 8.5")

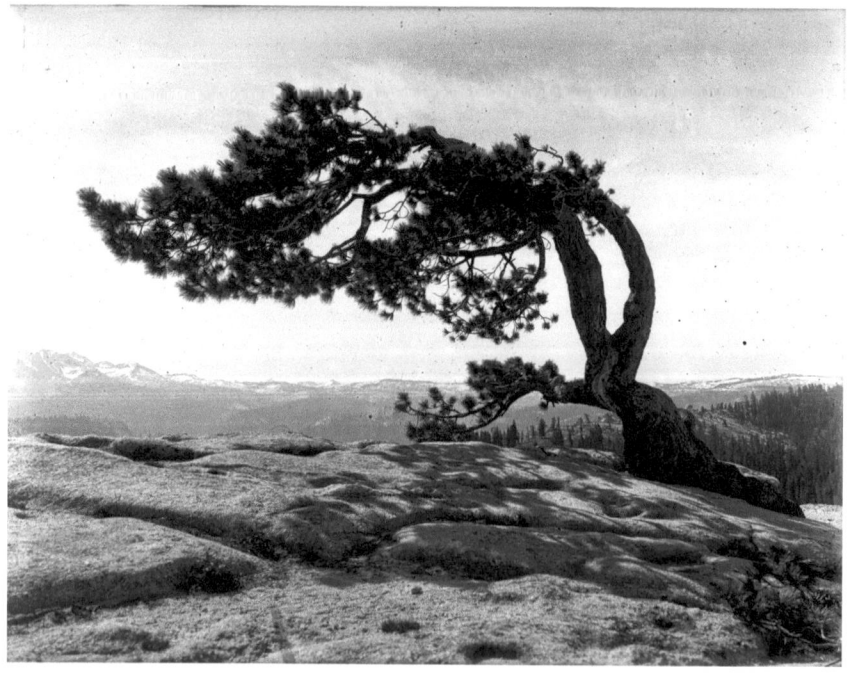

Sentinel Dome Tree (687, 6.5" x 8.5")

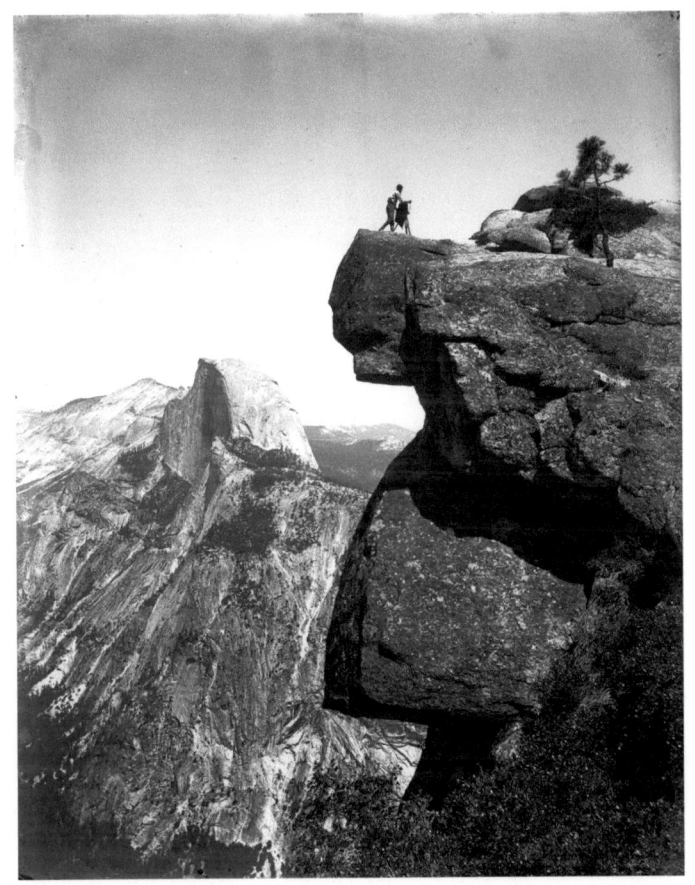

Photographer's Rock, View of Half Dome from Glacier Point (525, 8" x 10")

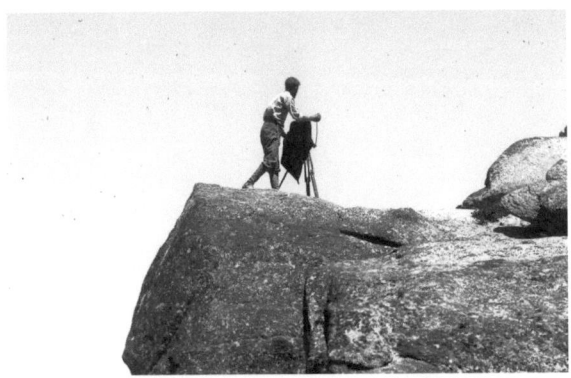

Detail of *Photographer's Rock* (525, 8" x 10")

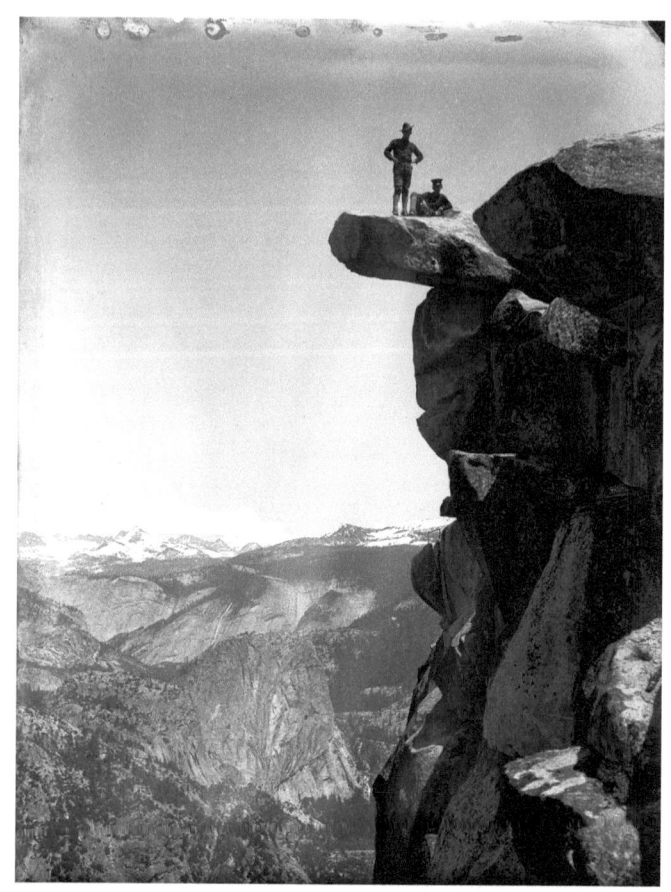

Overhanging Rock, Two Soldiers (Glacier Point) (603, 6.5" x 8.5")

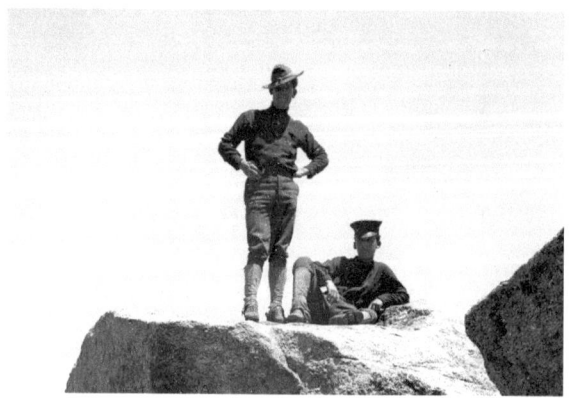

Detail of *Overhanging Rock, Two Soldiers* (603, 6.5" x 8.5")

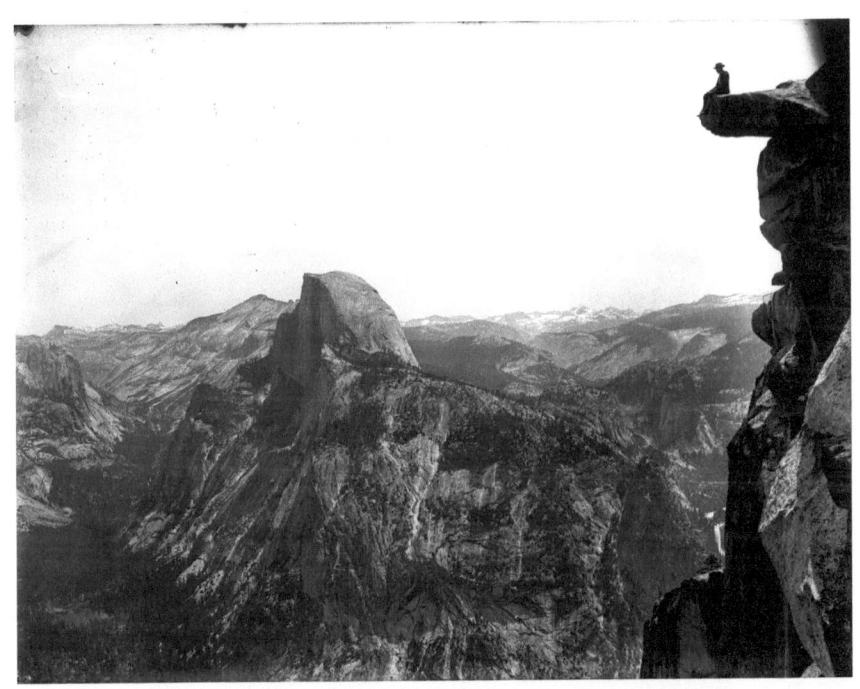

Overhanging Rock, Wide Angle (Glacier Point) (591, 6.5" x 8.5")

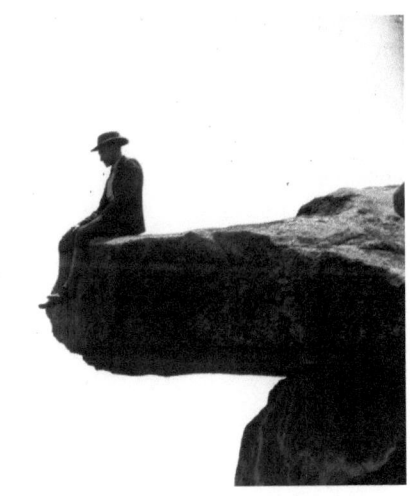

Detail of *Overhanging Rock, Wide Angle* (591, 6.5" x 8.5")

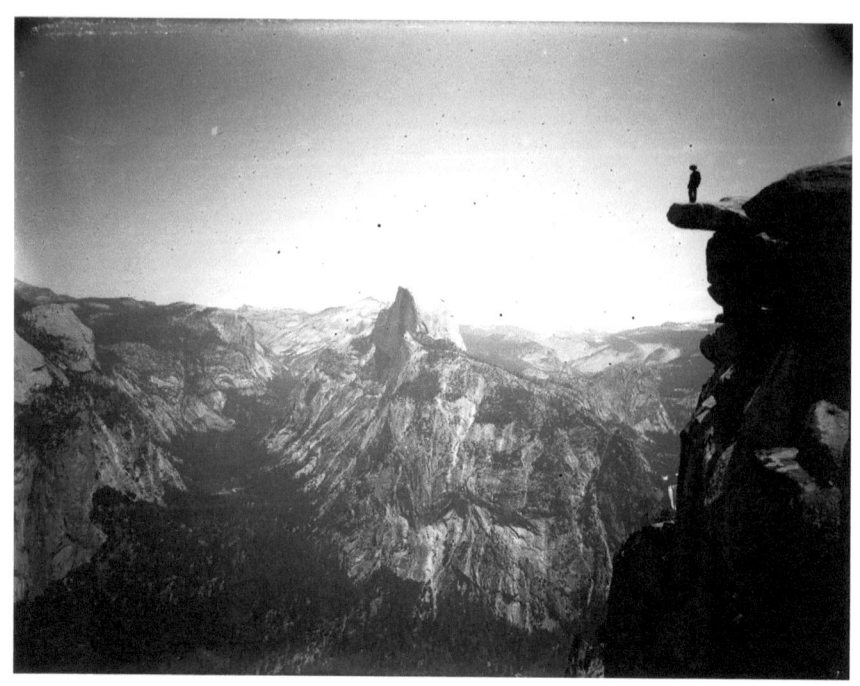

Overhanging Rock, Wide Angle (Glacier Point) (684, 6.5" x 8.5")

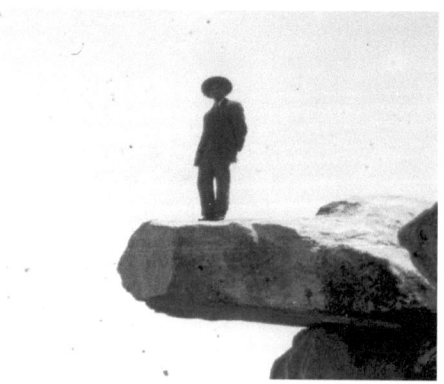

Detail of *Overhanging Rock, Wide Angle* (684, 6.5" x 8.5")

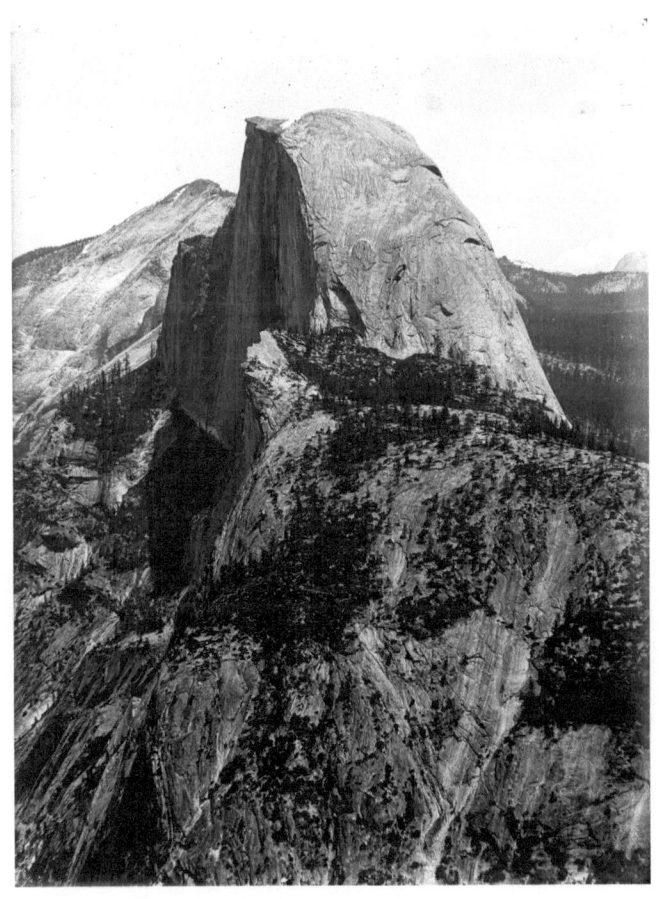

Half Dome from Glacier Point (590, 6.5" x 8.5")
Between Glacier Point and Washburn Point, along the road or trail.

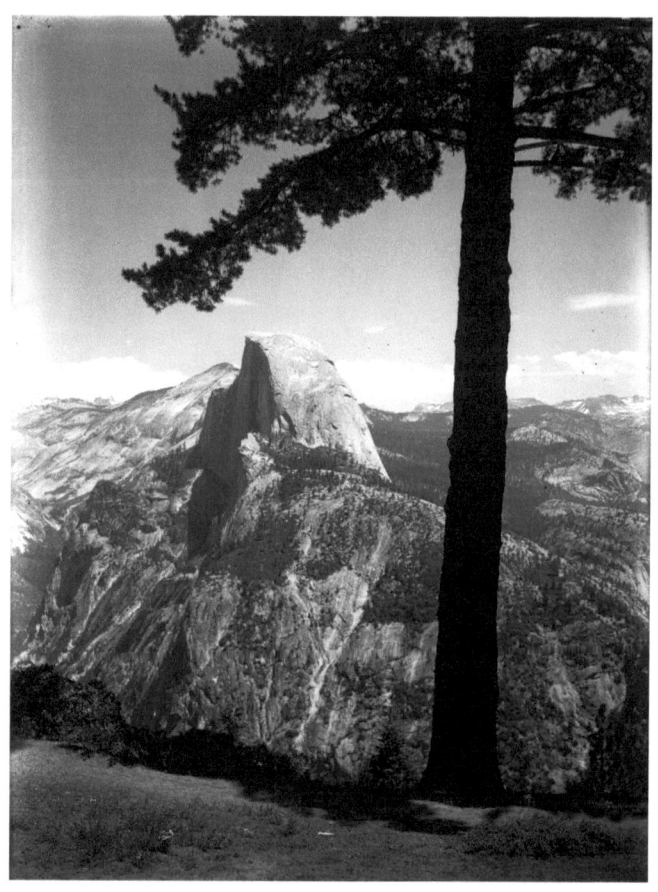

Tis-sa-ack, The Great Half Dome, from Washburn Point (683a, 6.5" x 8.5")

Legend tells how Tis-sa-ack with her tear-stained face, after a dispute with her husband, was transformed into the rock we now know as Half Dome.

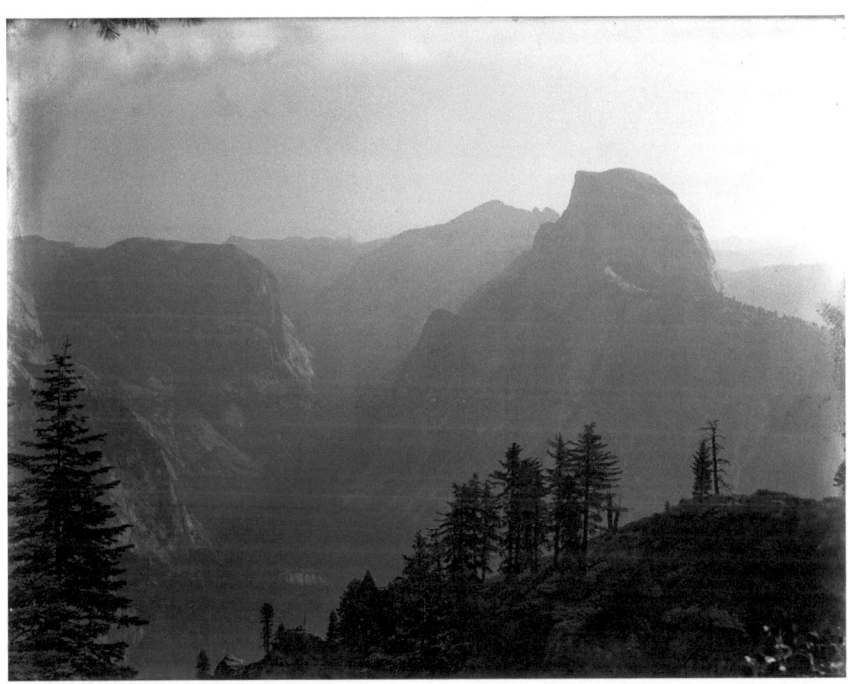

Half Dome from Glacier Point Trail (581, 6.5" x 8.5")

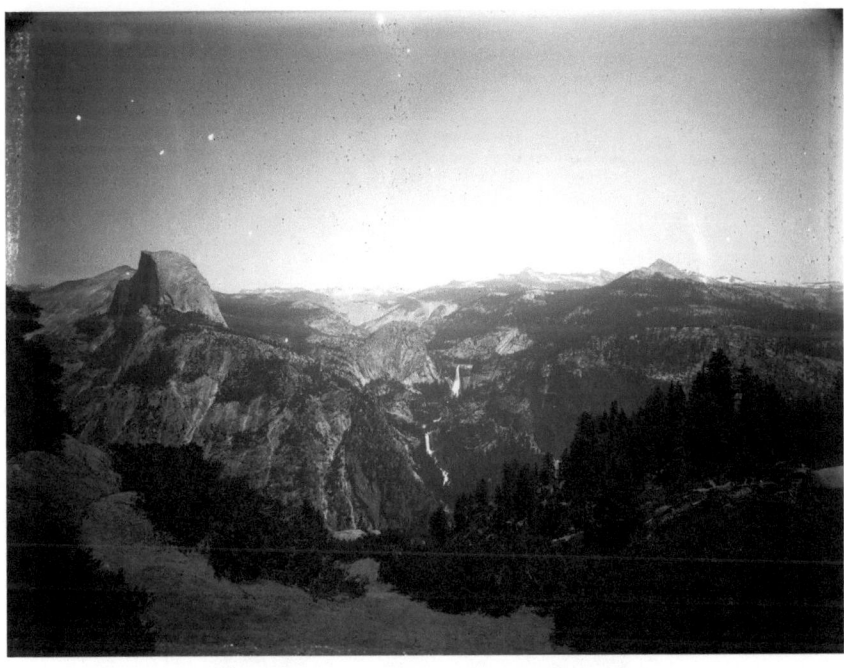

Glacier Point Panorama (685, 6.5" x 8.5")
Between Glacier Point and Washburn Point, along the road or trail.

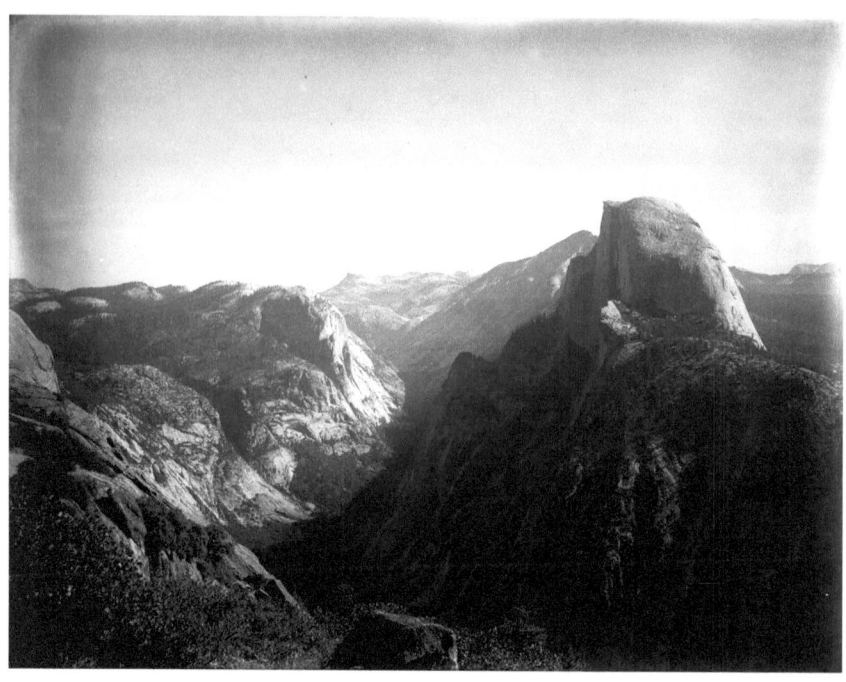

Tenaya Canyon, Early Morning (653, 6.5" x 8.5")

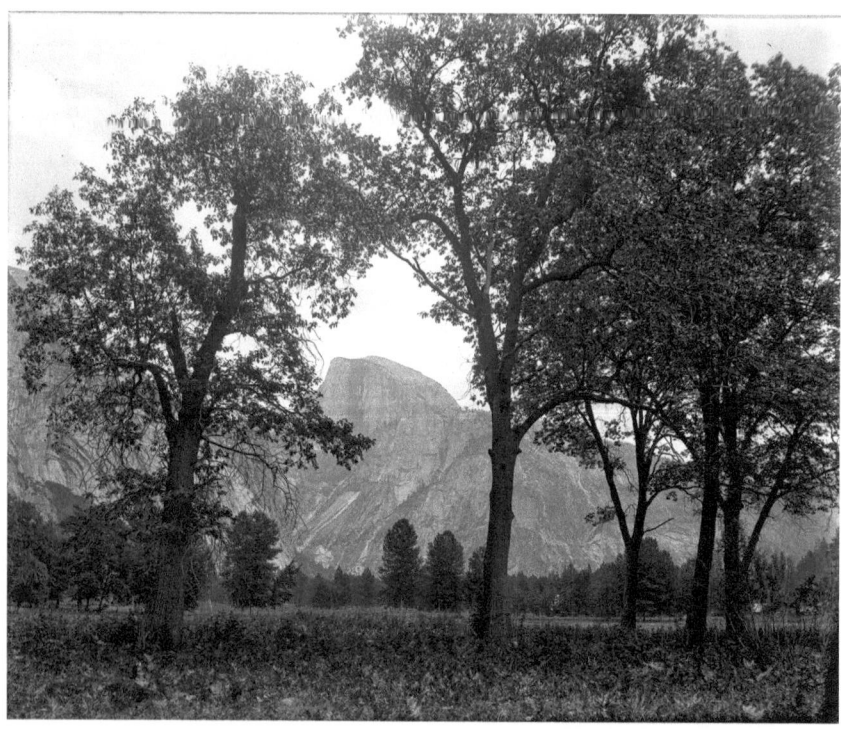

Half Dome from Meadow (526, 8" x 10")

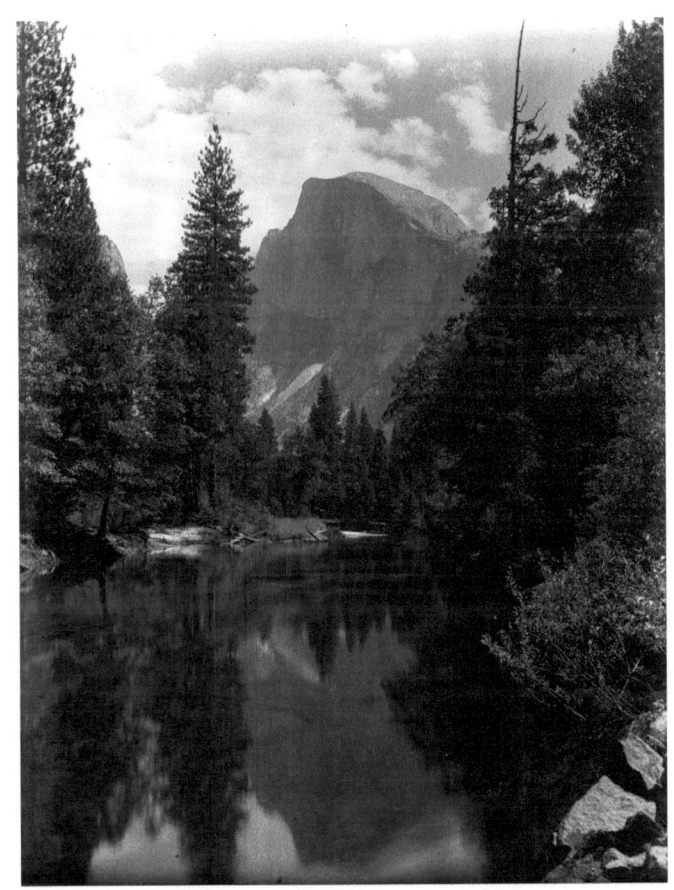

Half Dome and River (649, 6.5" x 8.5")

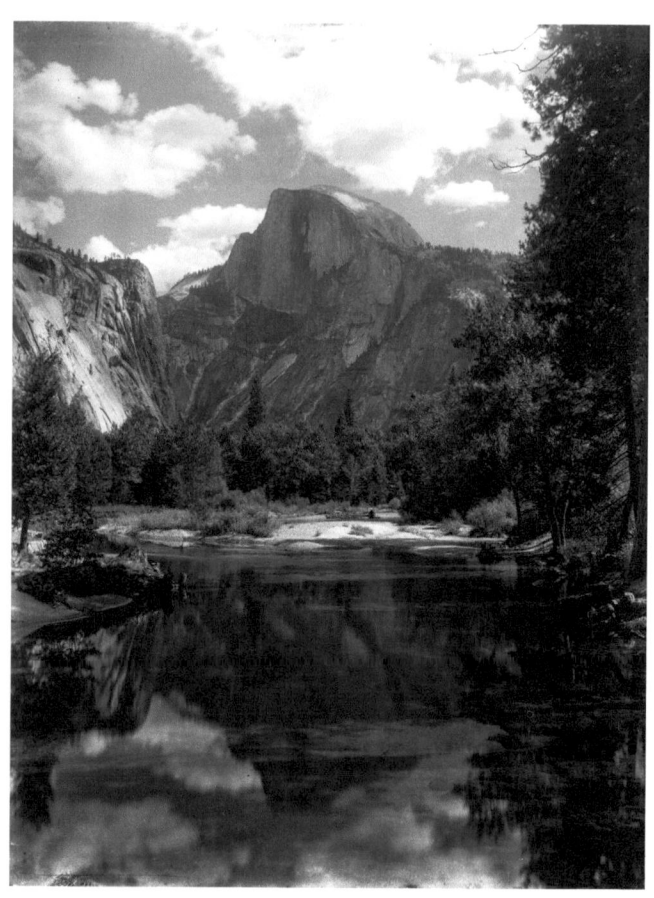

Half Dome from Bridge (665, 6.5" x 8.5")

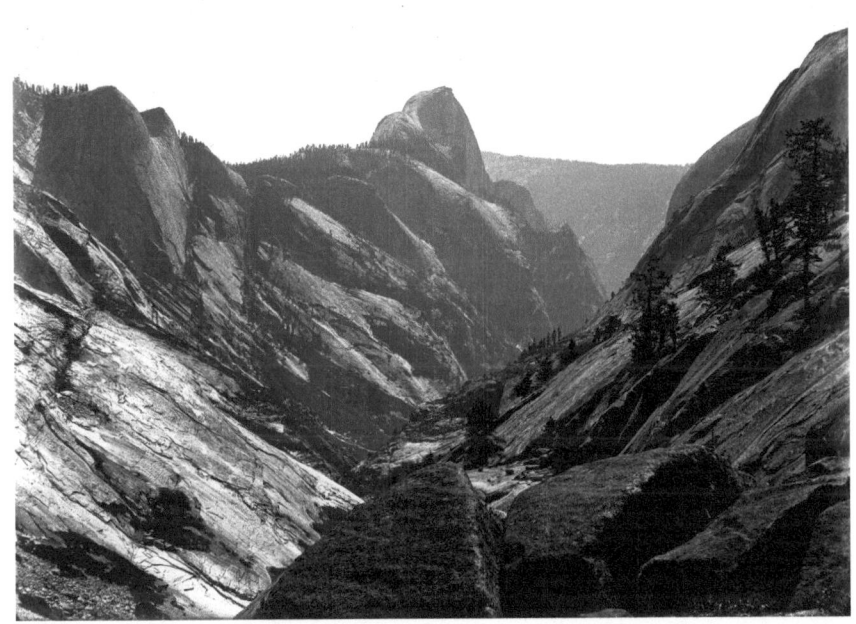

Half Dome from the Head of Tenaya Canyon (601, 6.5" x 8.5")

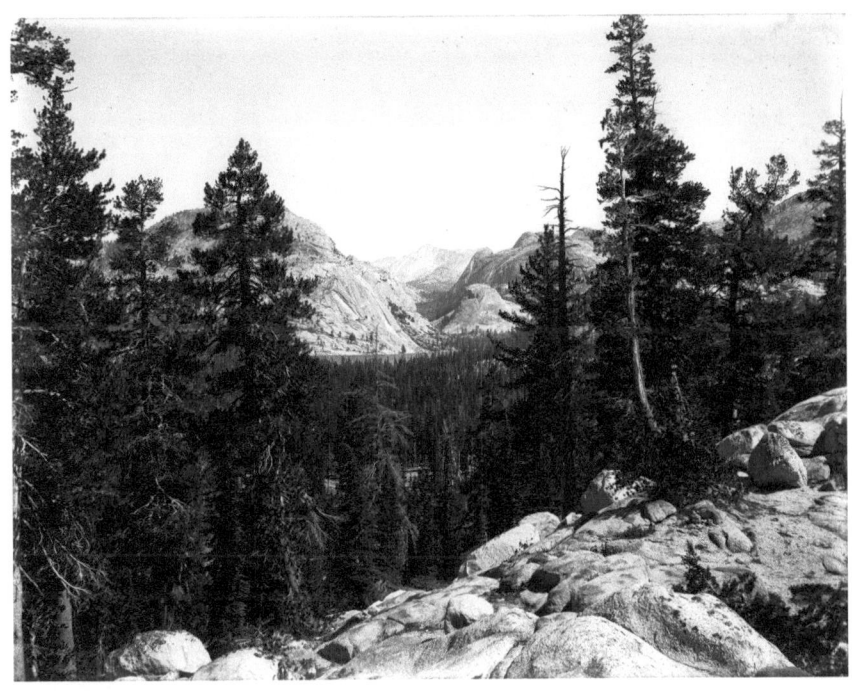

Mt. Conness and Tenaya Lake (606, 6.5" x 8.5")

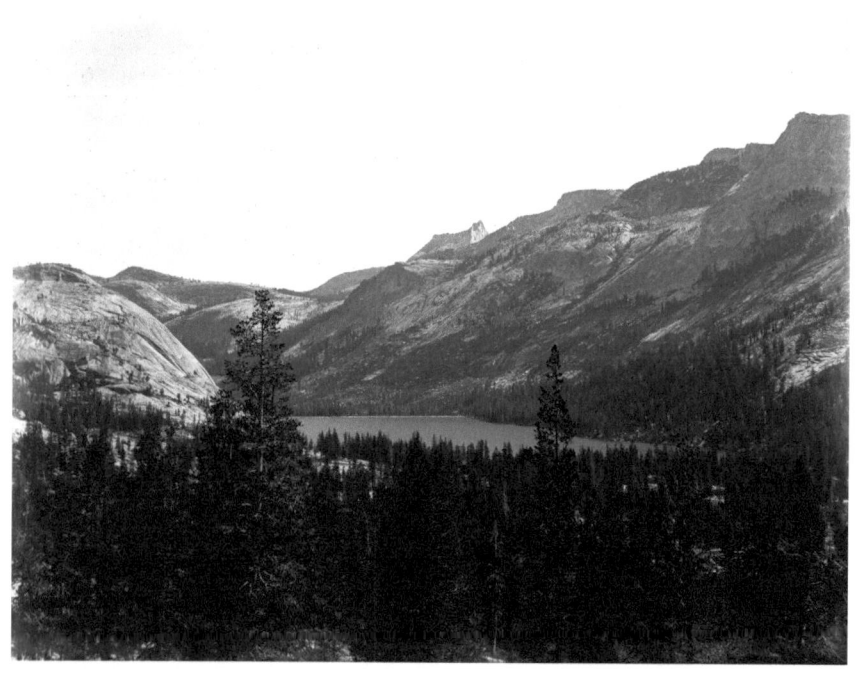

Tenaya Lake and Cathedral Peak (608, 6.5" x 8.5")

Lakes, rivers, and Streams

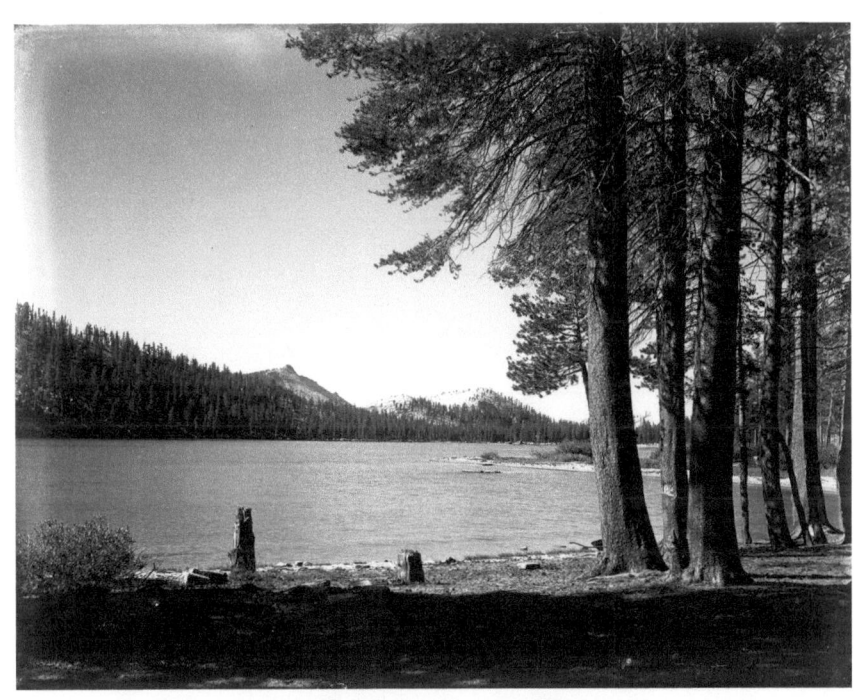

Tenaya Lake Showing Clouds Rest (548, 6.5" x 8.5")

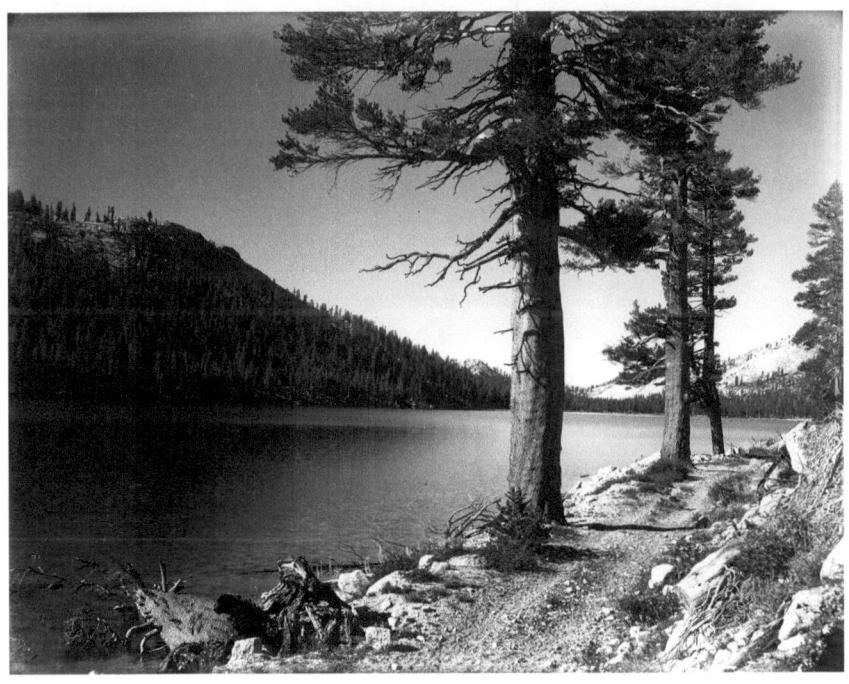

Tenaya Lake from Northeast Shore (607, 6.5" x 8.5")

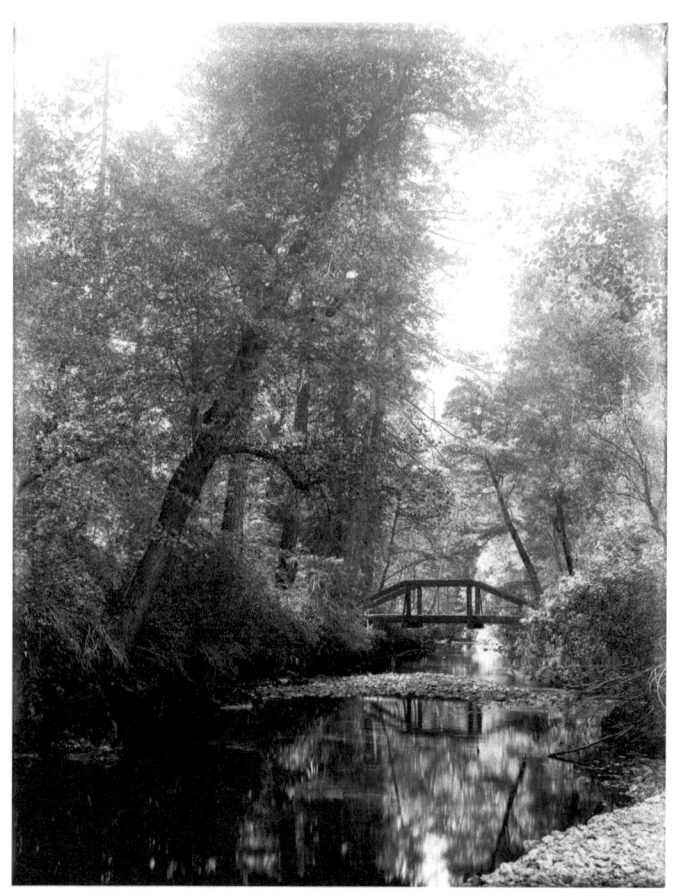

Tenaya Creek Study with Bridge (655, 6.5" x 8.5")

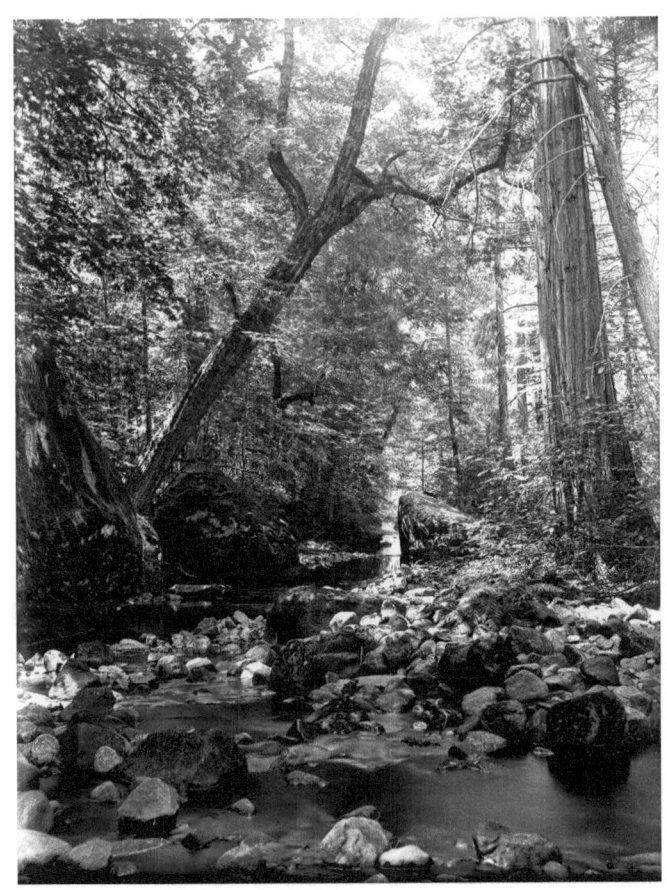
Tenaya Creek Study (549, 6.5" x 8.5")

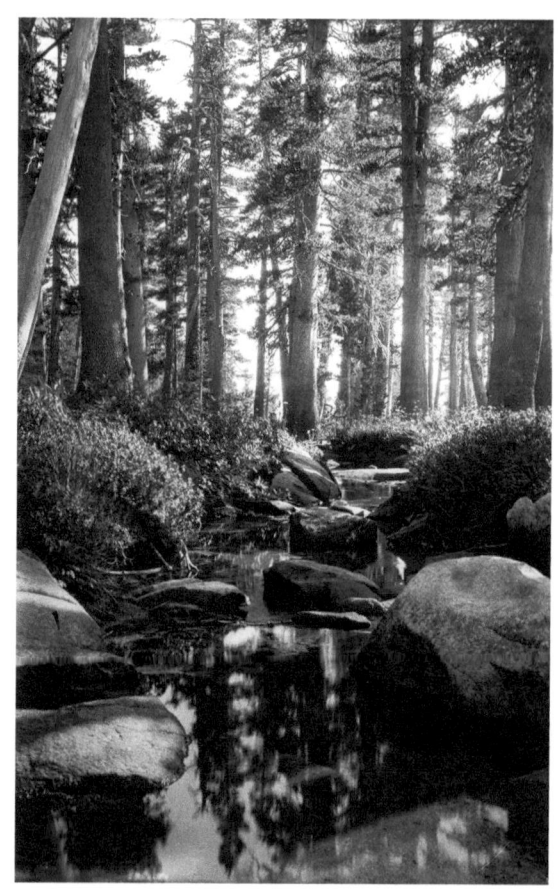

Creek Study (619, 6.5" x 8.5")

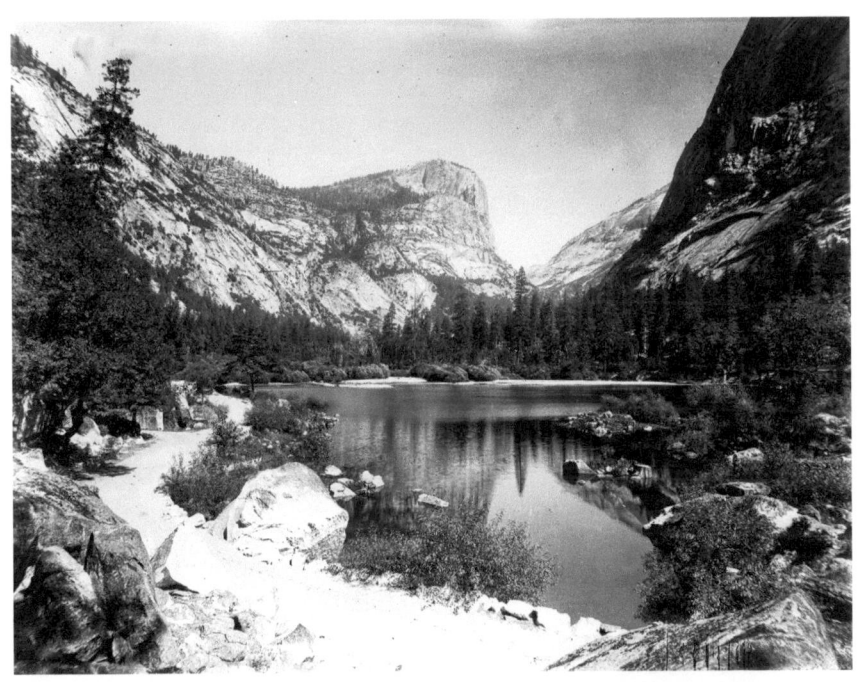

Mirror Lake, Showing Road (545, 6.5" x 8.5")

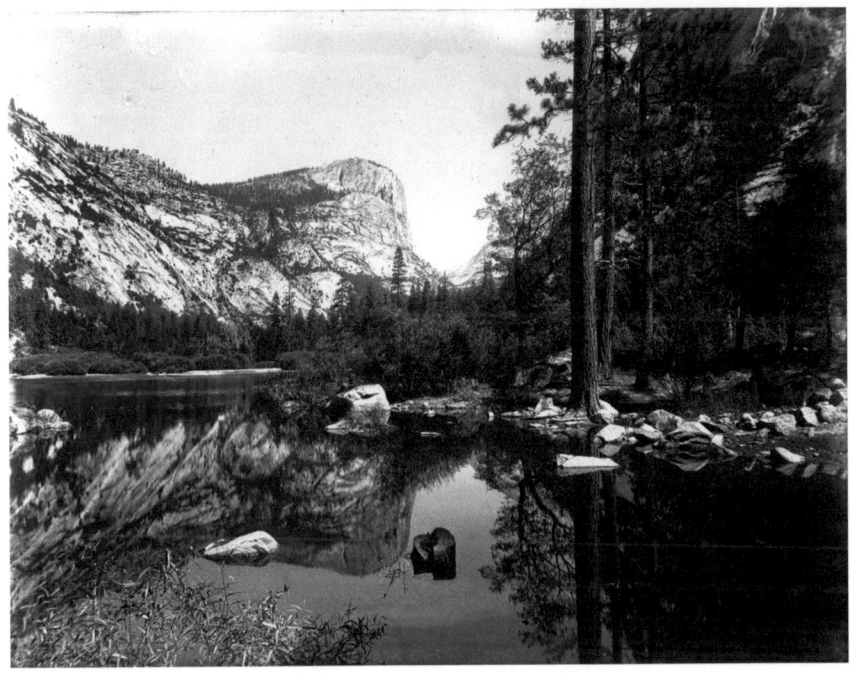

Mirror Lake Landscape (598, 6.5" x 8.5")

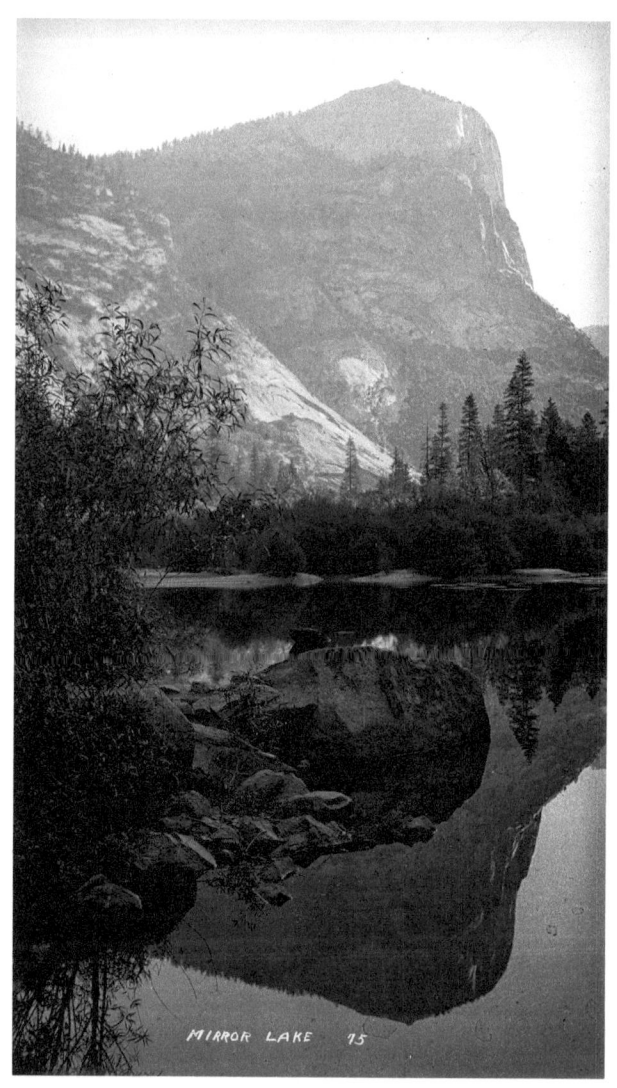

Mirror Lake with Reflection of Mt. Watkins (403, 5" x 7")

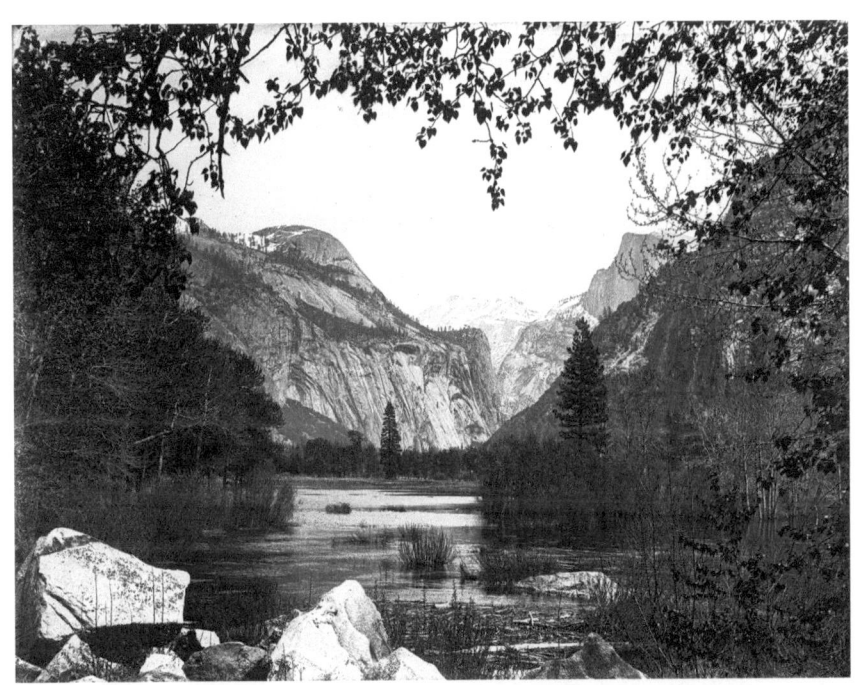

Domes from Rocky Point, Leafy Bower (506a, 6.5" x 8.5")

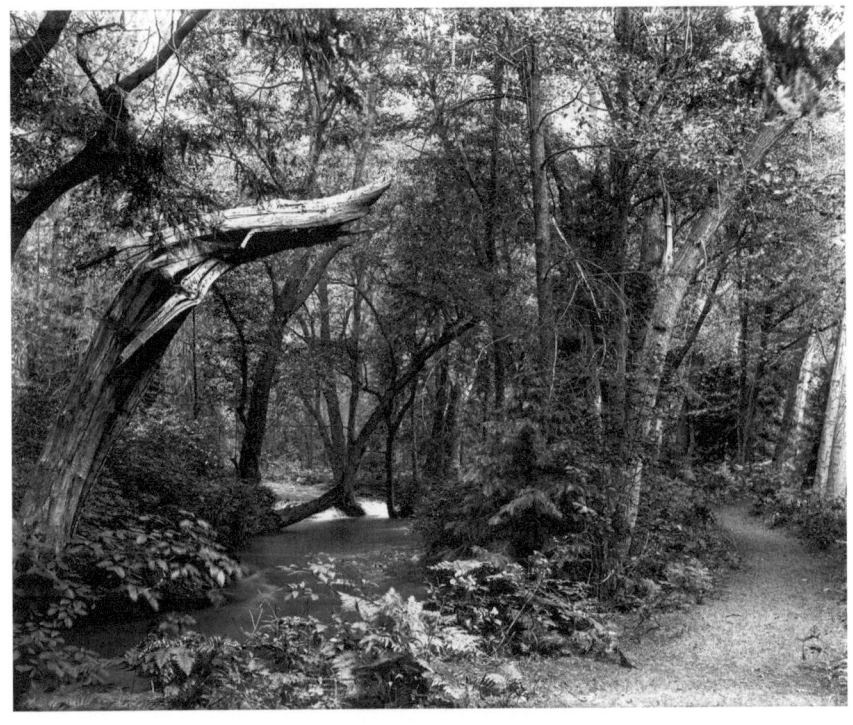

Lost Arrow Trail, Yosemite Creek (529, 8" x 10")

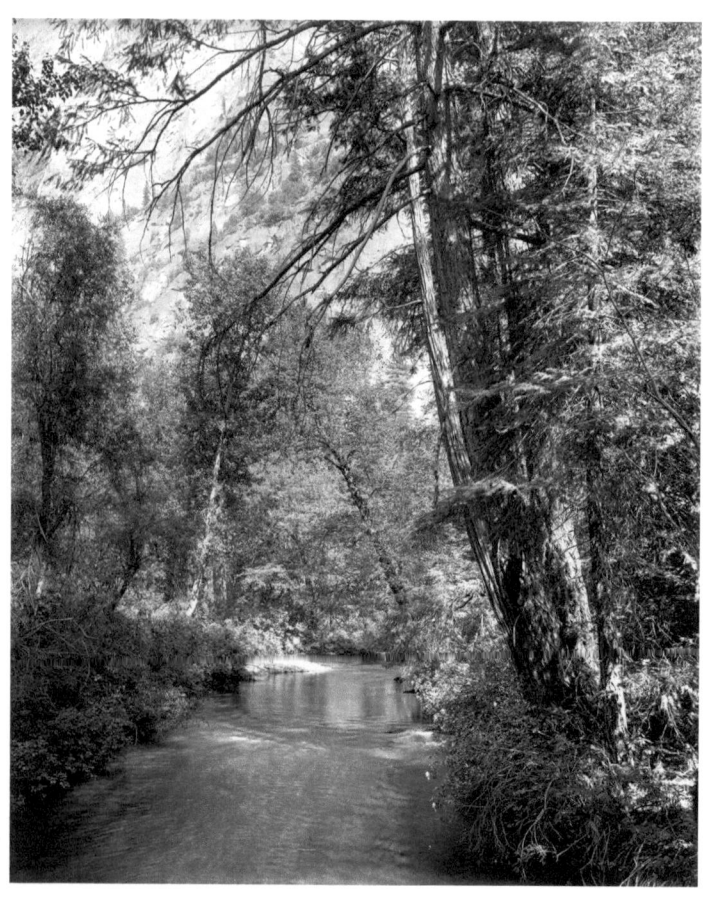

The Bank of the Stream (544b, 8" x 10")
Yosemite Creek, morning.

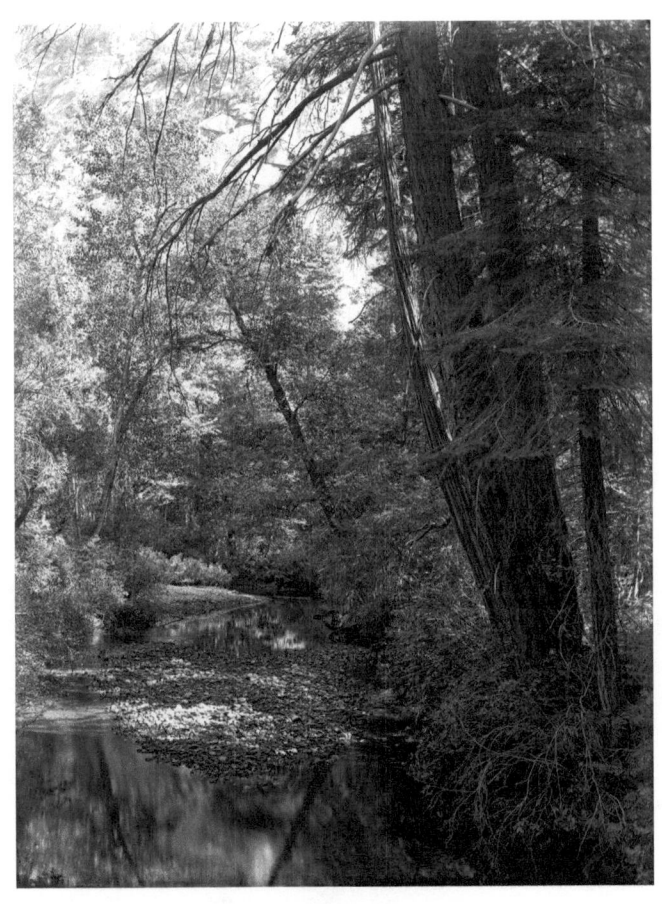

Stream Bank (654, 6.5" x 8.5")
Yosemite Creek, mid-day.

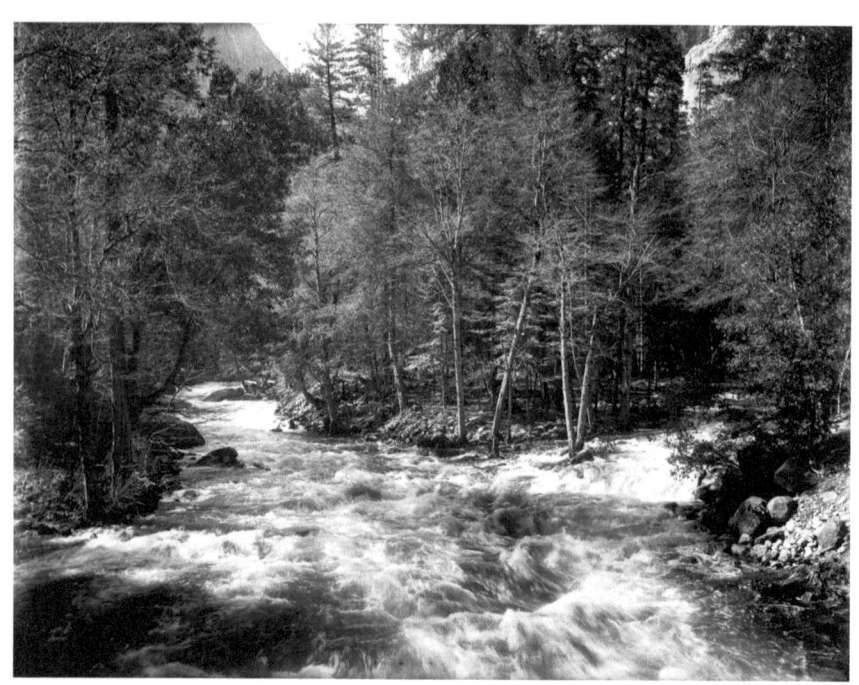

Meeting of the Waters, Happy Isles, High Water (656, 6.5" x 8.5")

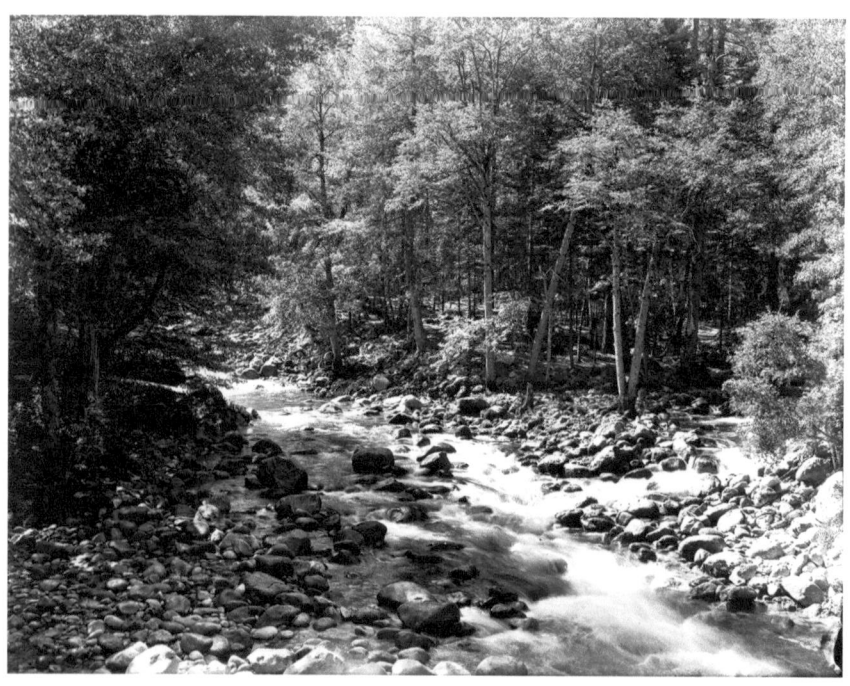

Meeting of the Waters, Happy Isles, Low Water (594, 6.5" x 8.5")

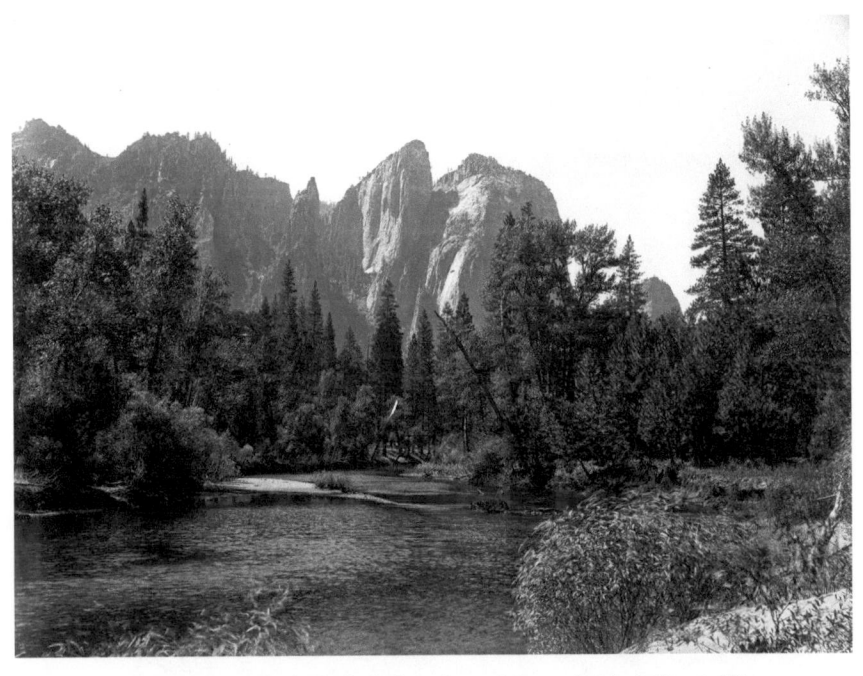

Merced River with Cathedral Rocks and Spires (554, 6.5" x 8.5")

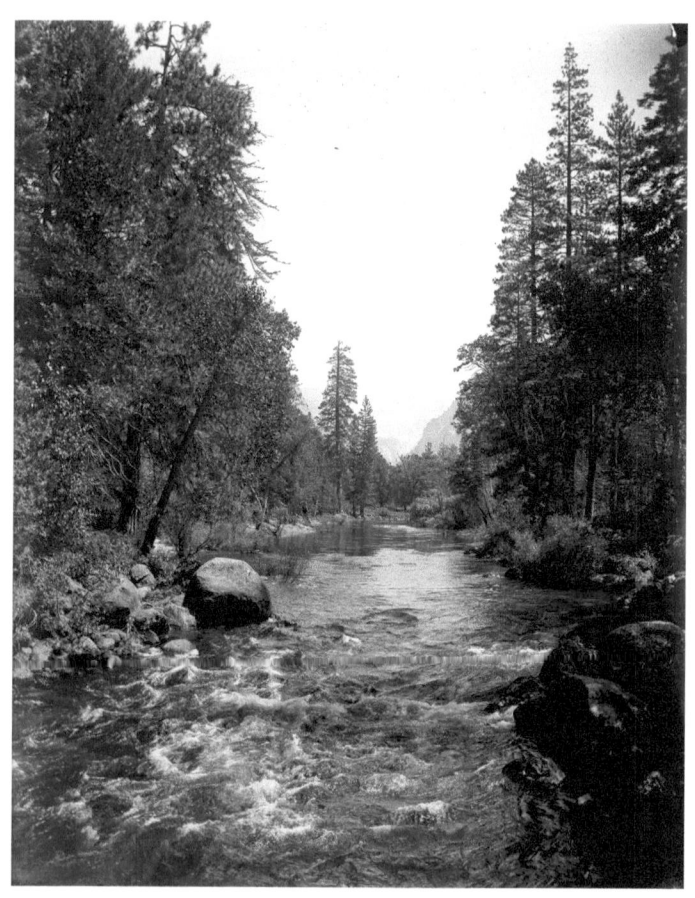

Merced River from El Capitan Bridge (541, 8" x 10")

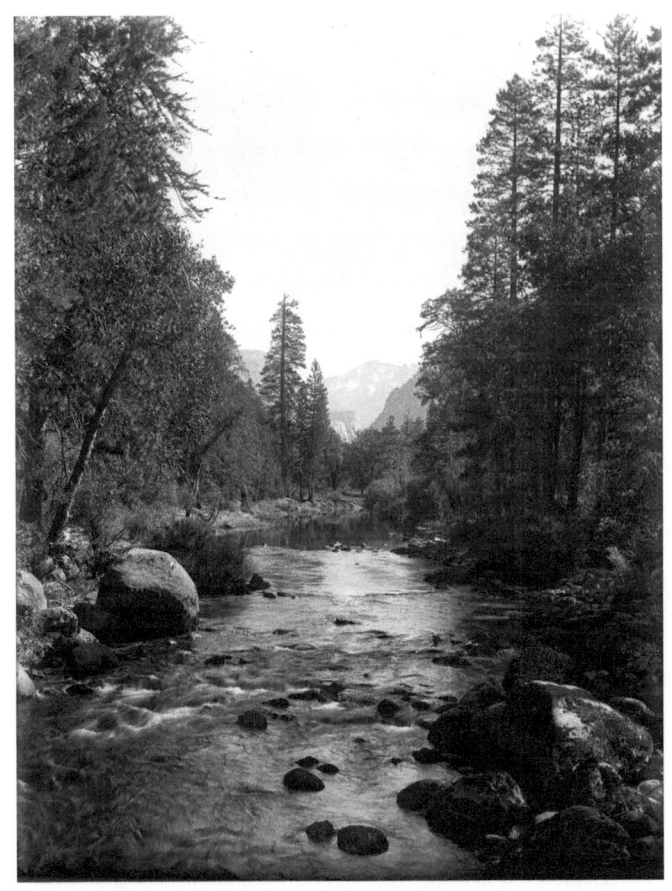

Merced River from El Capitan Bridge, Low Water (546, 6.5" x 8.5")

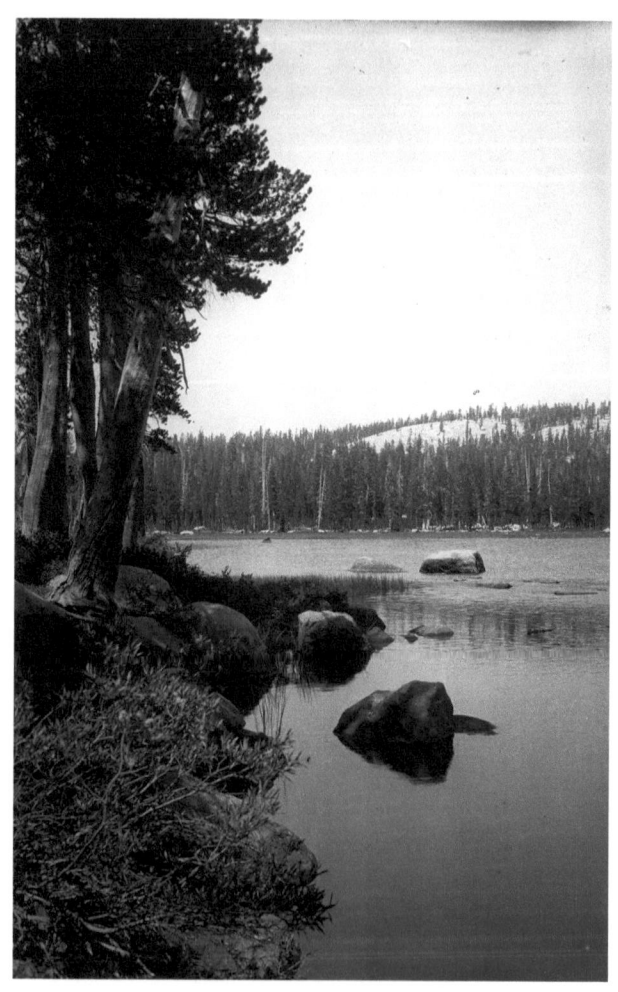

Crescent Lake, East of Wawona (620, 6.5" x 8.5")

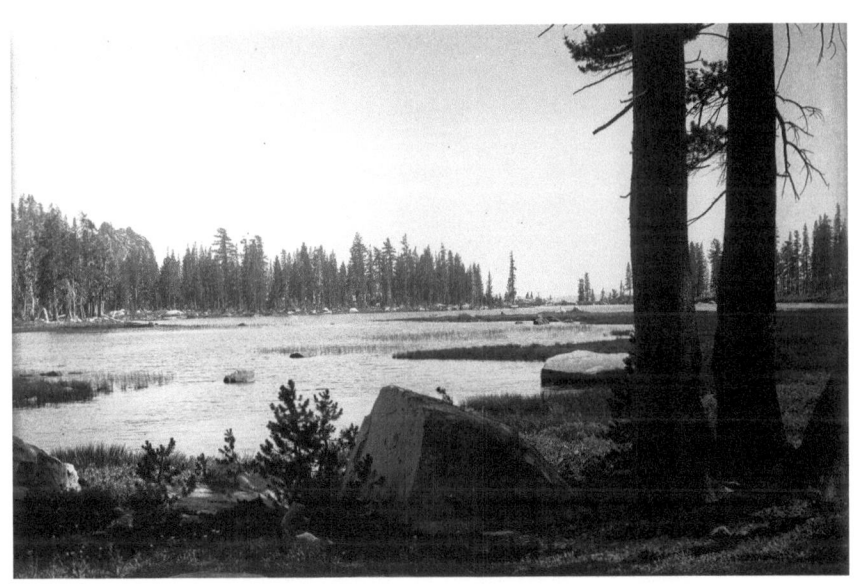

Crescent Lake, East of Wawona (623, 6.5" x 8.5")

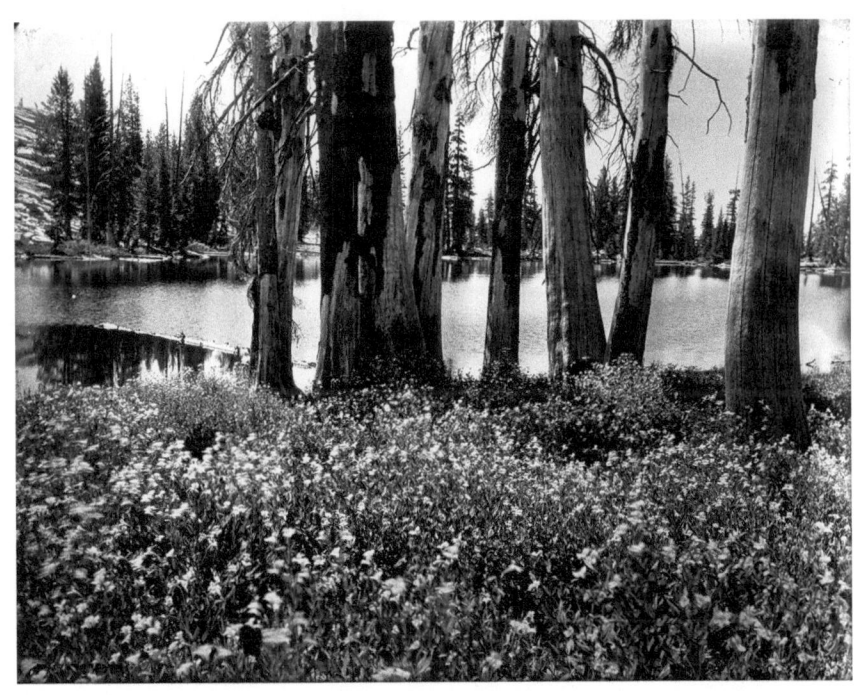

Minnow Lake with Pink Mimulus *(Monkey-flower), East of Wawona*
(621, 6.5" x 8.5")

Sequoias

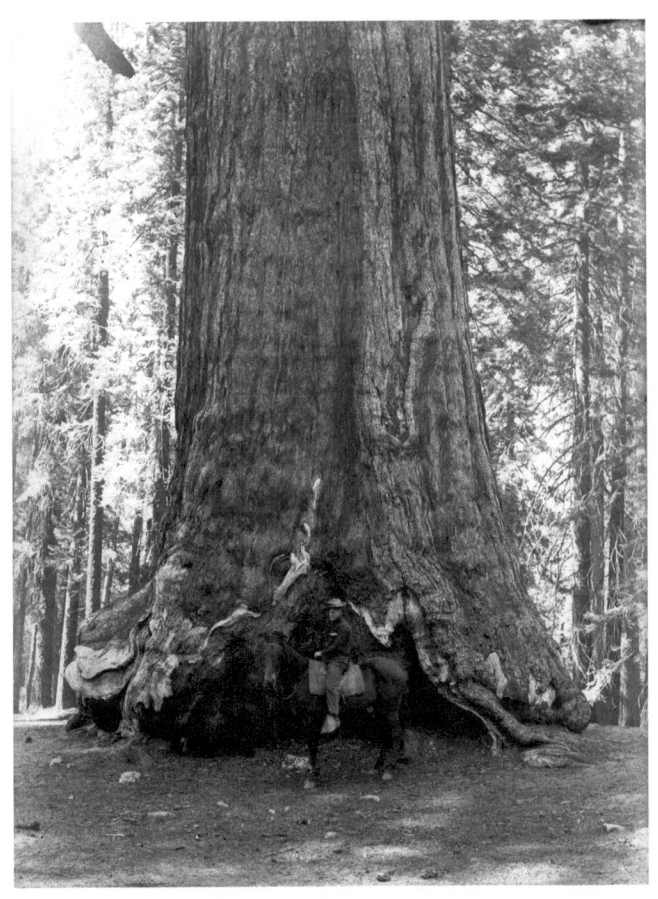

Grizzly Giant Base with Ranger (1510, 6.5" x 8.5")

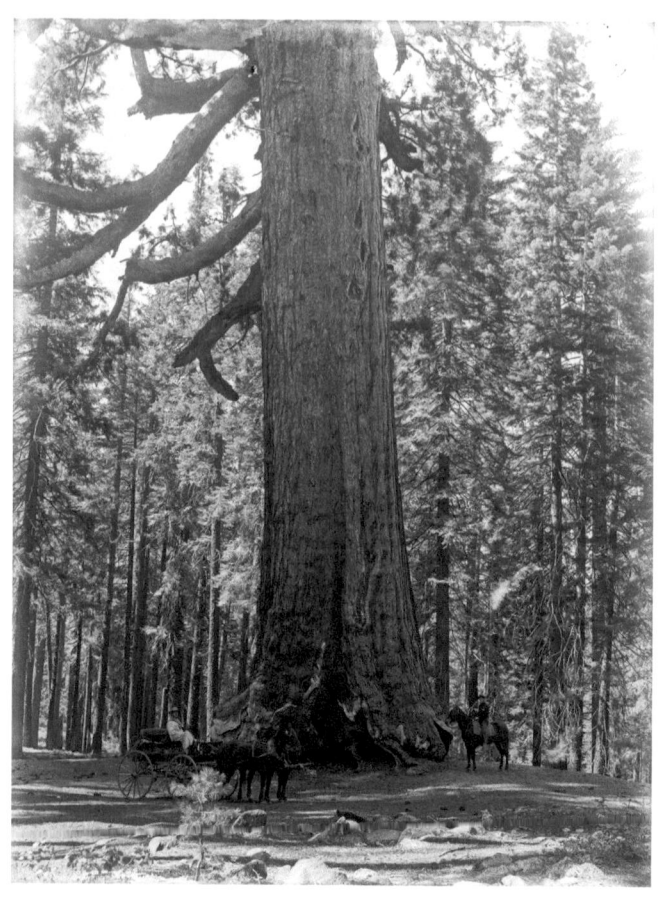

Grizzly Giant Base with Carriage and Ranger (1576, 6.5" x 8.5")

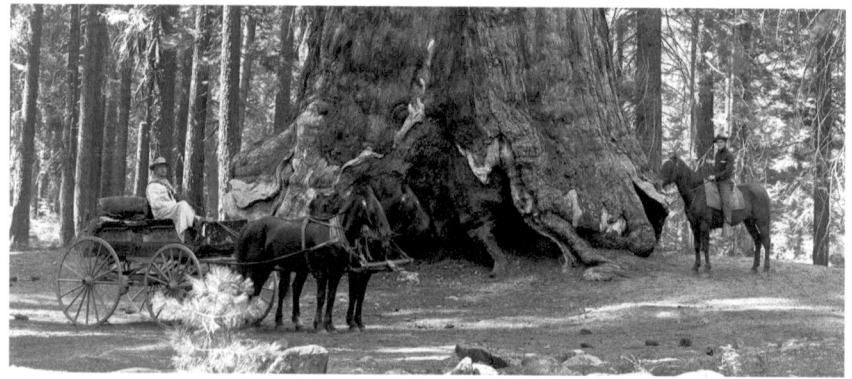

Detail of *Grizzly Giant Base with Carriage and Ranger* (1576, 6.5" x 8.5")

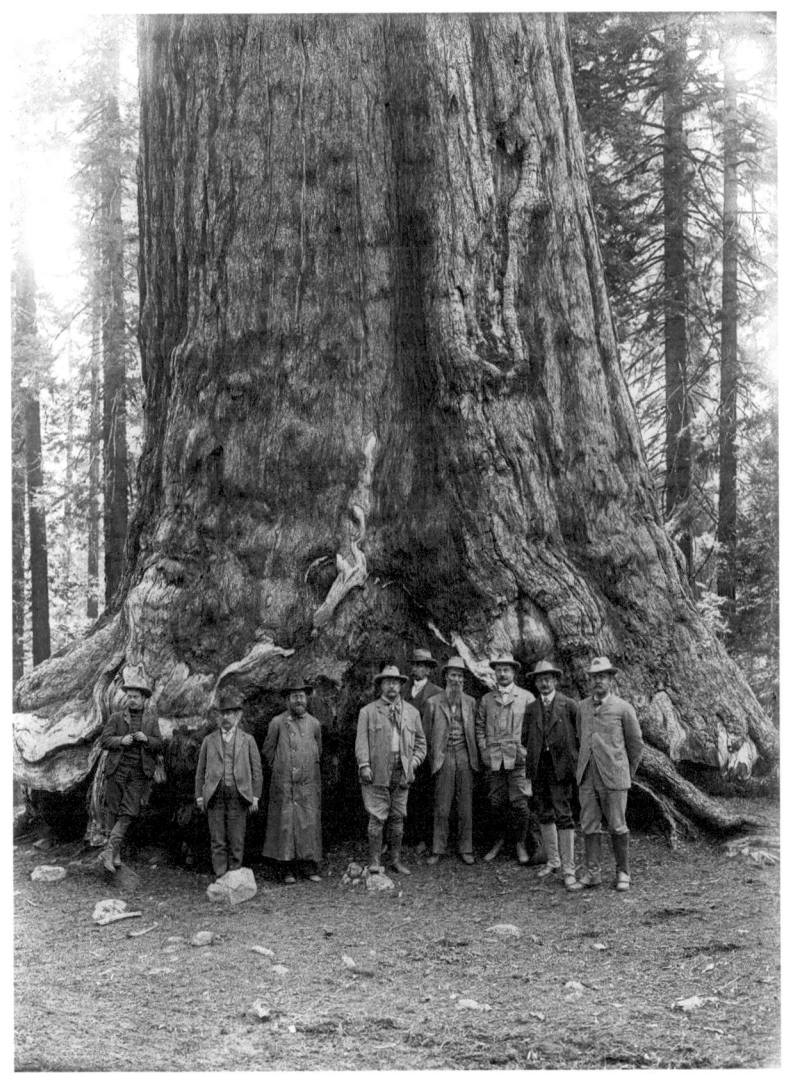

Grizzly Giant with Roosevelt Party (1504, 6.5" x 8.5")

May 15, 1903. From left: secret service man; Secretary of the Navy William H. Moody; CA Governor George C. Pardee; President Theodore Roosevelt; Dr. Presley M. Rixey, surgeon general; John Muir; Nicholas Murray Butler, president of Columbia University; William Loeb Jr., Roosevelt's private secretary; and Benjamin Ide Wheeler, president of the University of CA

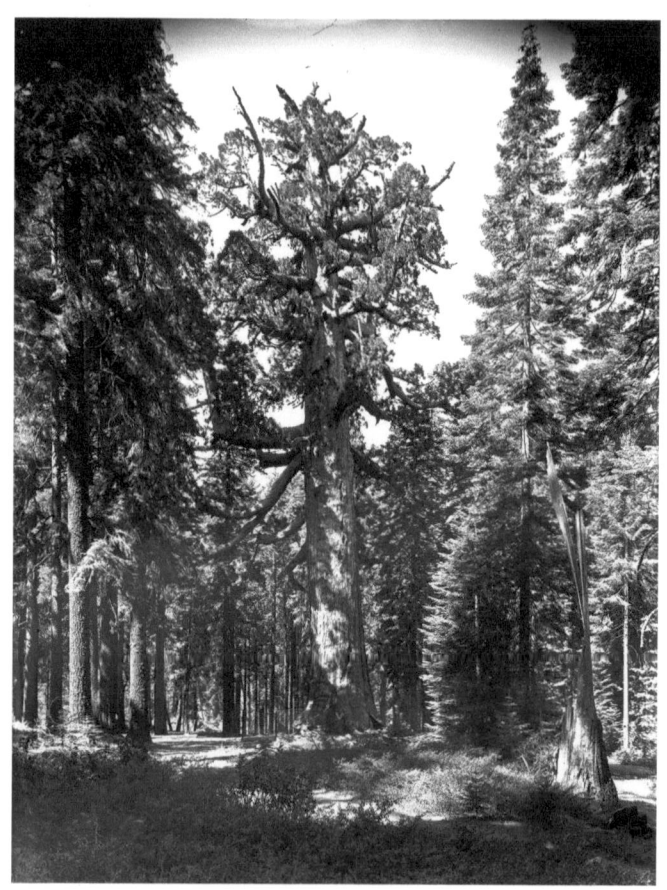

Grizzly Giant (1530, 6.5" x 8.5")

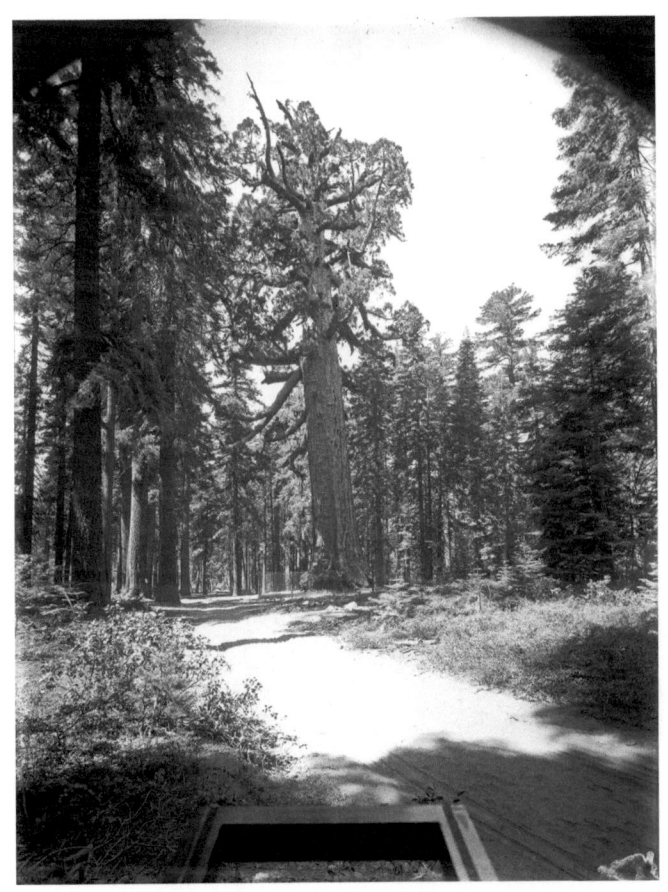

Grizzly Giant with Camera Stand (1532, 6.5" x 8.5")

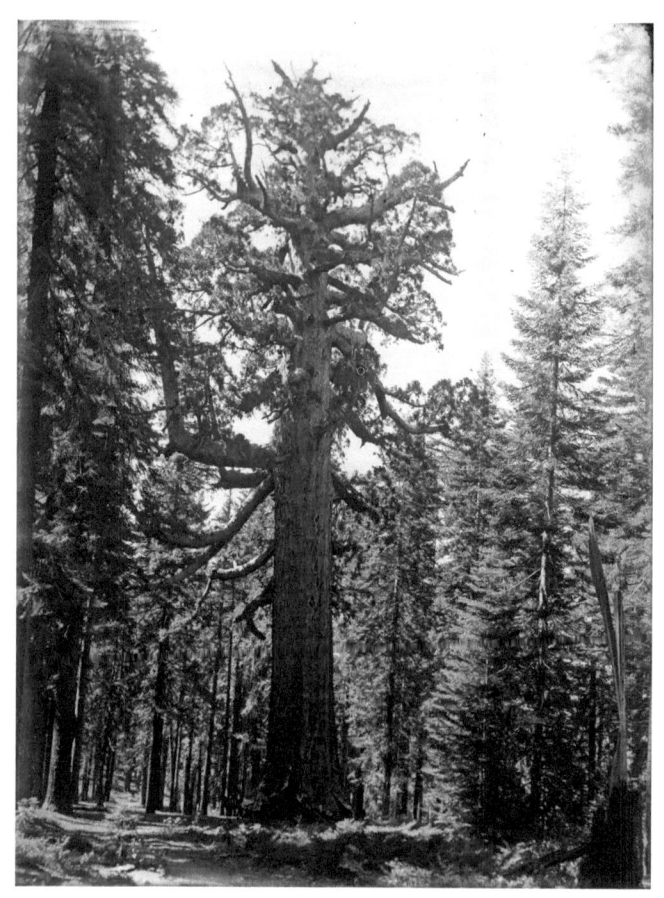

Grizzly Giant with Ranger at Base (1508, 6.5" x 8.5")

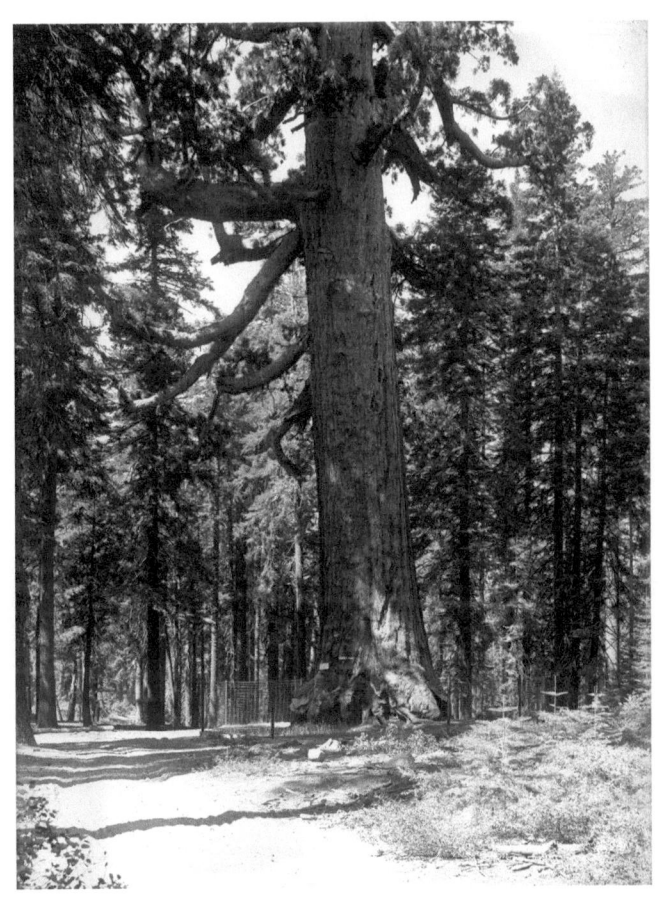

Grizzly Giant Trunk with Fence (1531, 6.5" x 8.5")

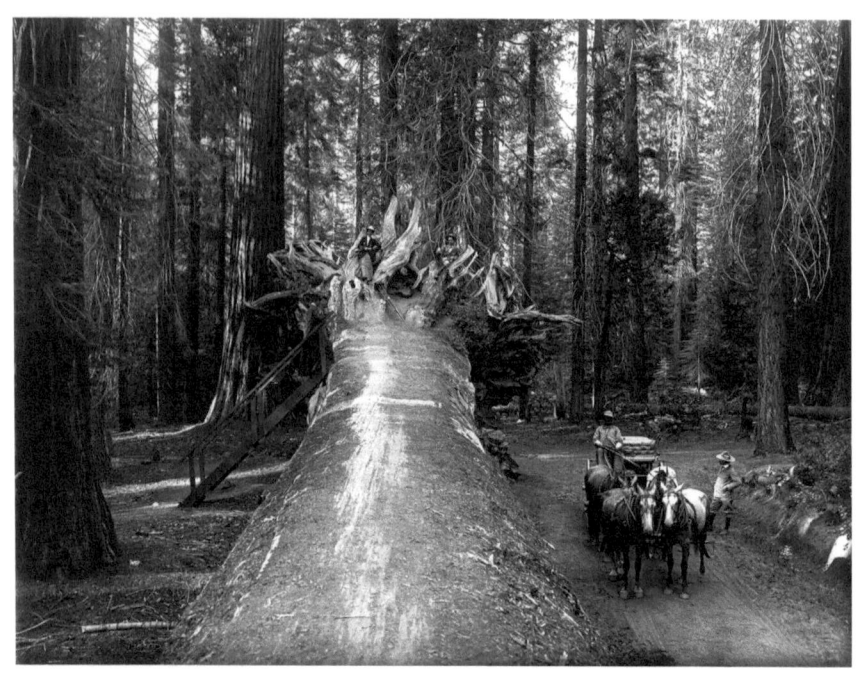

Fallen Monarch with Stairs, Carriage, and People (15XX, 6.5" x 8.5")

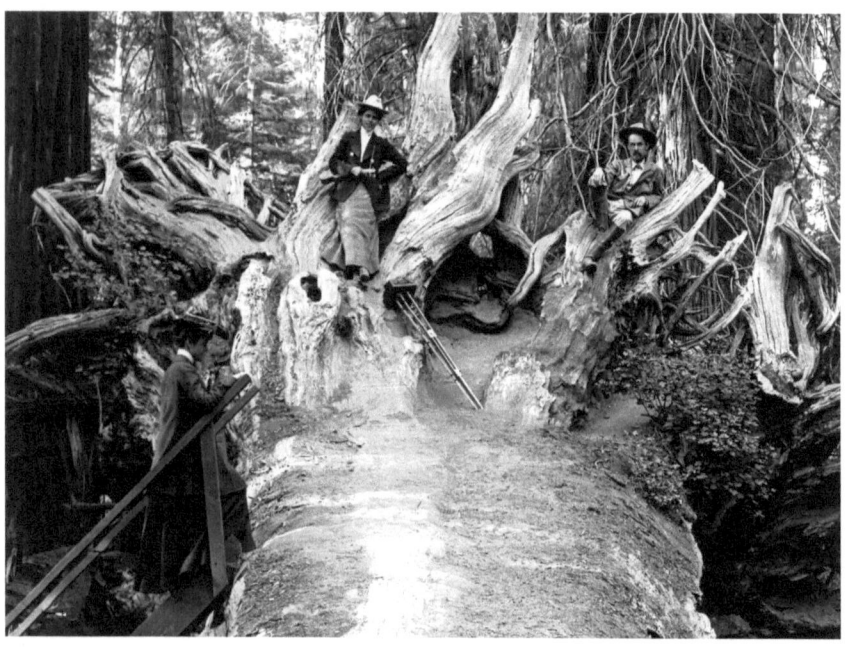

Detail of *Fallen Monarch with Stairs, Carriage, and People* (15XX, 6.5" x 8.5")

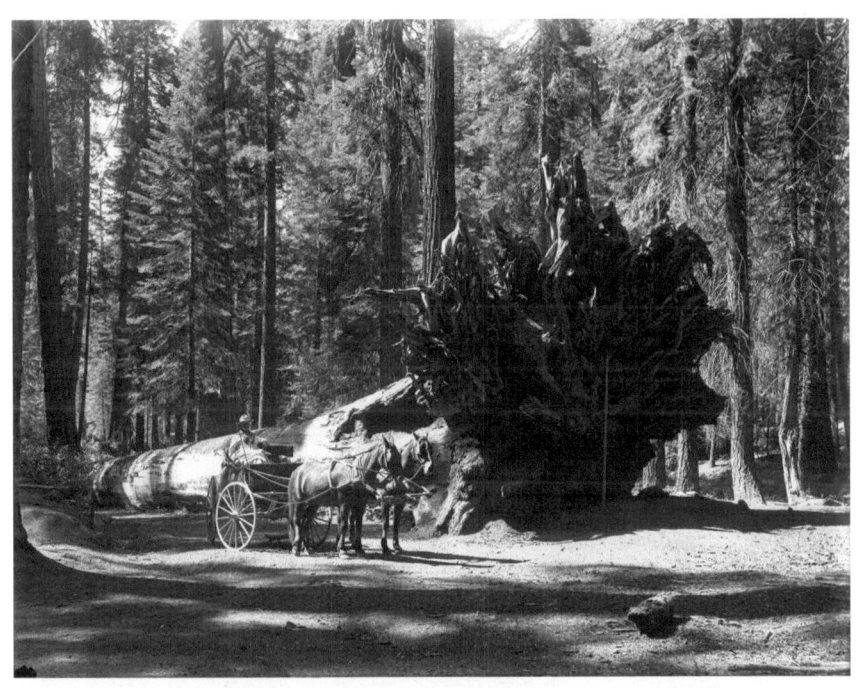

Fallen Monarch with Carriage (1503, 6.5" x 8.5")

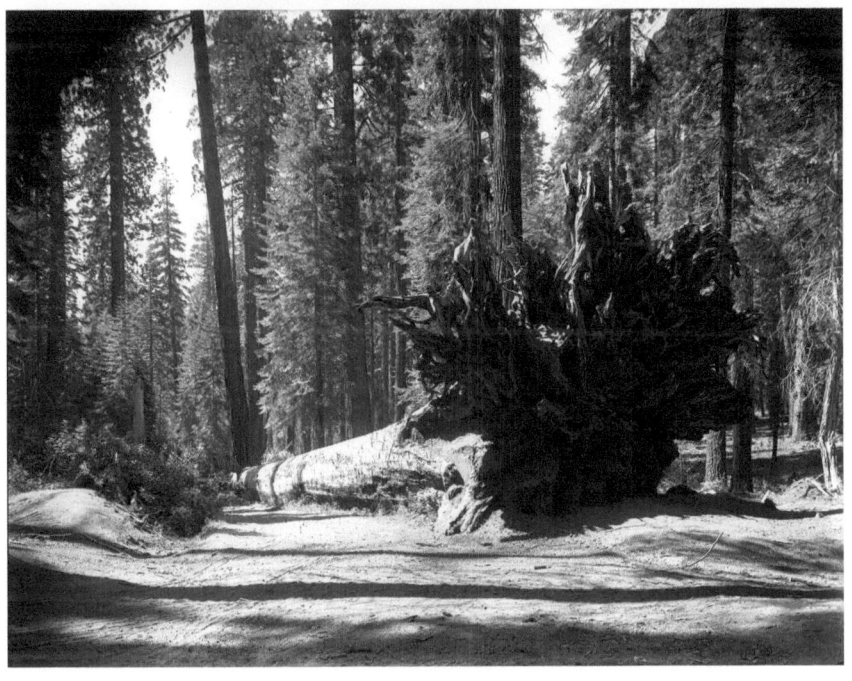

Fallen Monarch (1525, 6.5" x 8.5")

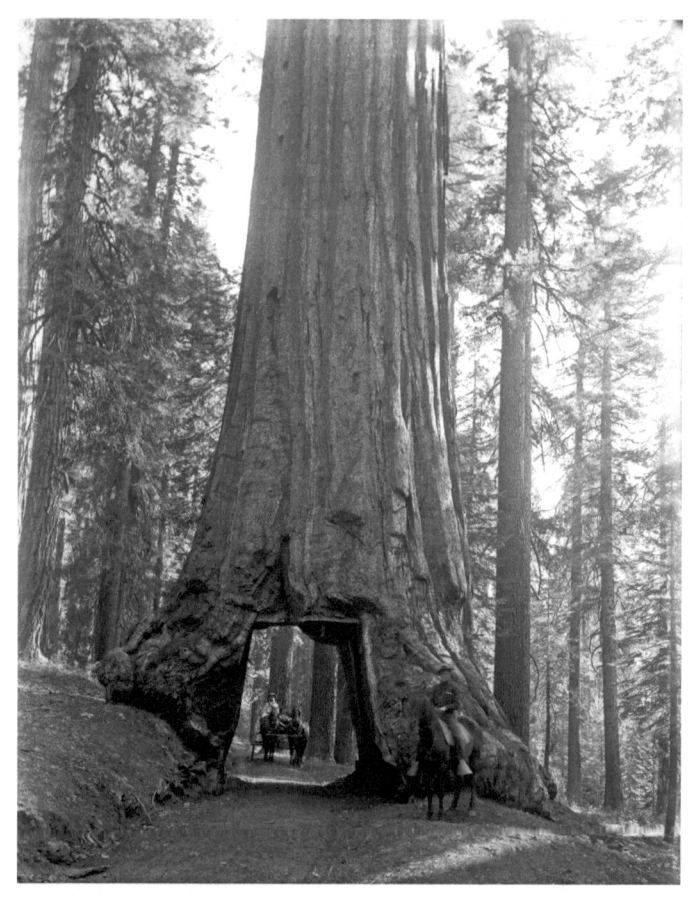

Wawona Tree with Carriage and Ranger (1521, 6.5" x 8.5")

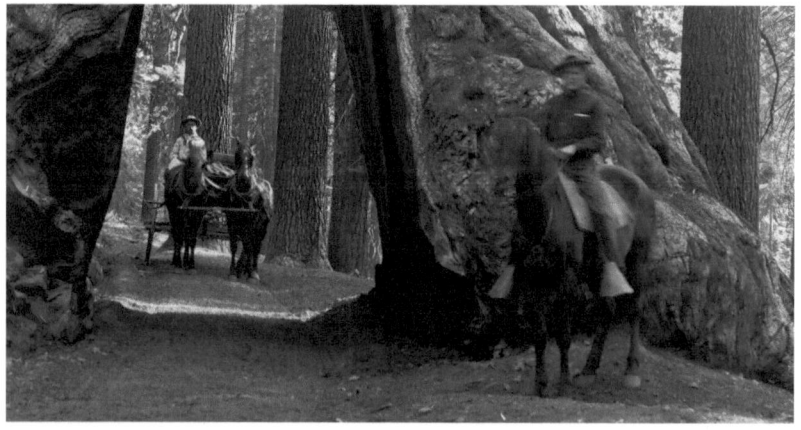

Detail of *Wawona Tree with Carriage and Ranger* (1521, 6.5" x 8.5")

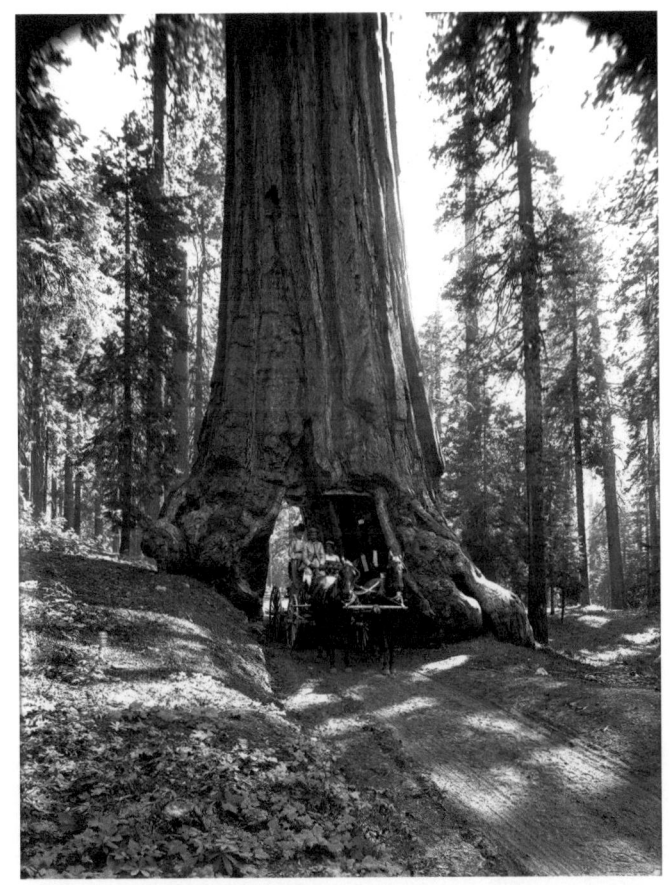

Wawona Tree with Carriage (1554, 6.5" x 8.5")

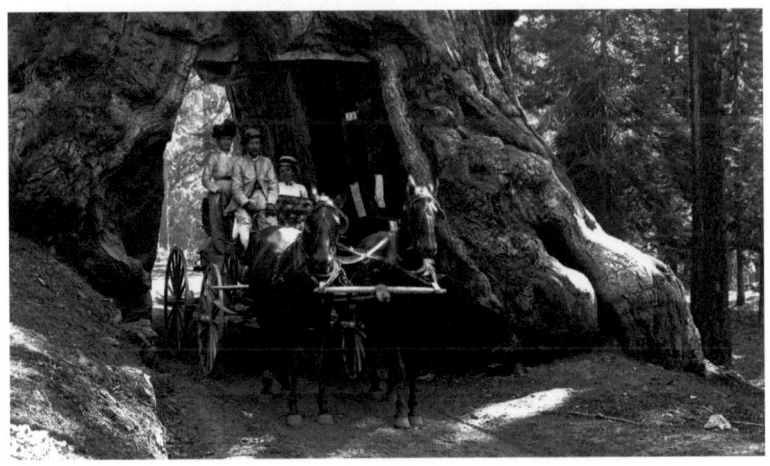

Detail of *Wawona Tree with Carriage* (1554, 6.5" x 8.5")

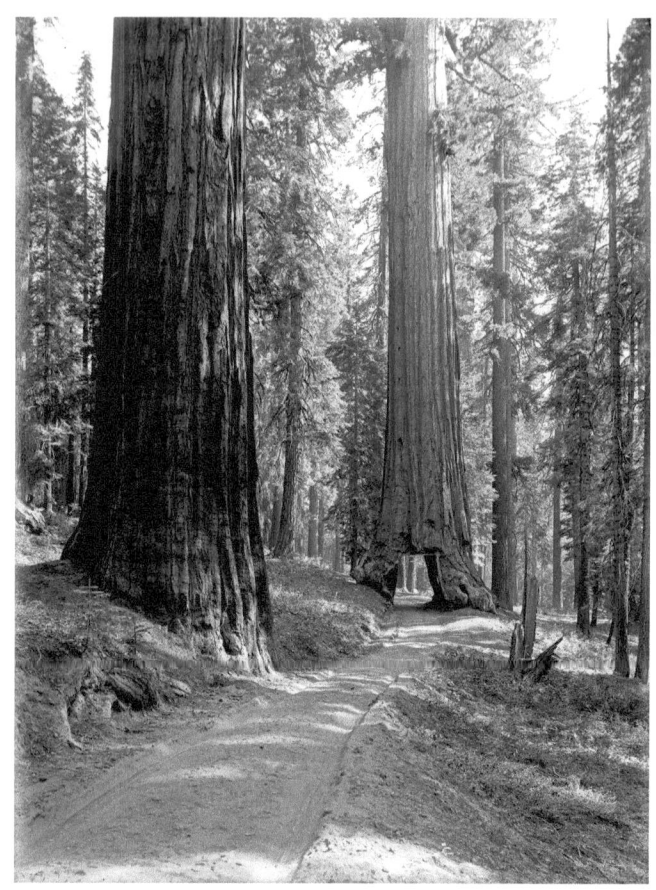

Vermont and Wawona Trees (1555, 6.5" x 8.5")

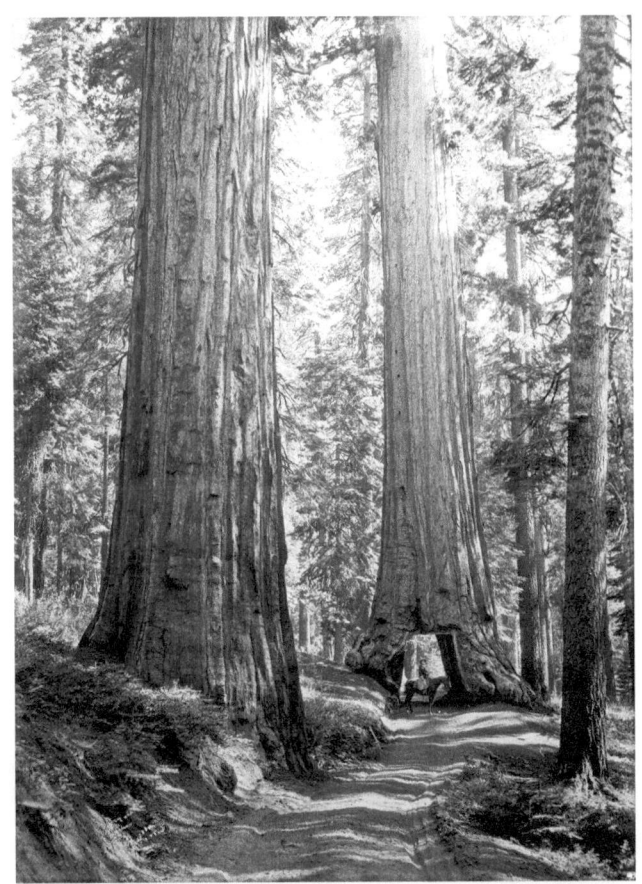

Vermont and Wawona Trees with Rider (1519, 6.5" x 8.5")

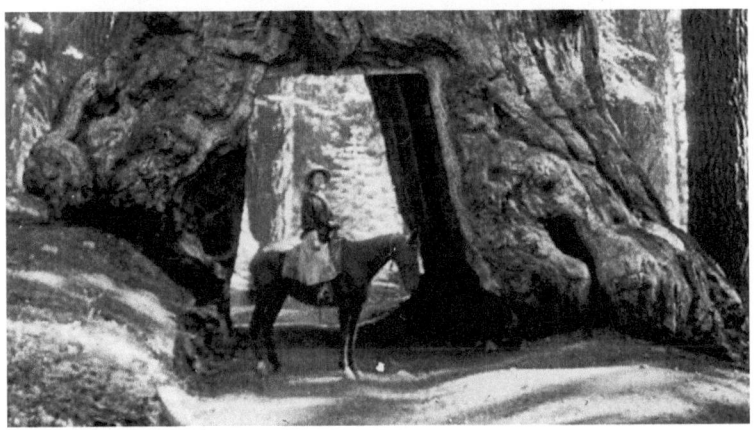

Detail of *Vermont and Wawona Trees with Rider* (1519, 6.5" x 8.5")

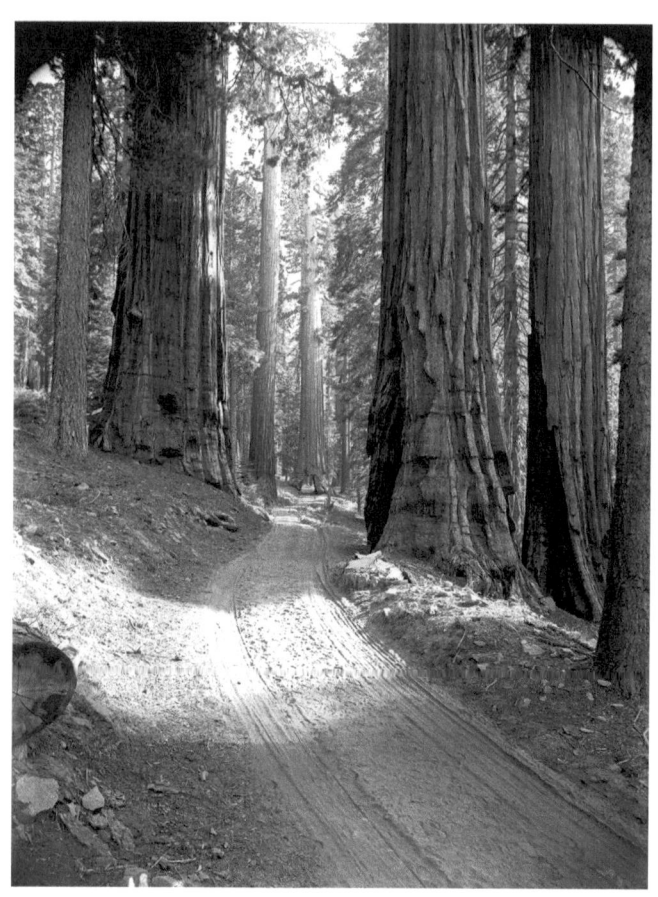

Vermont and Wawona Trees, Road Study (1556, 6.5" x 8.5")

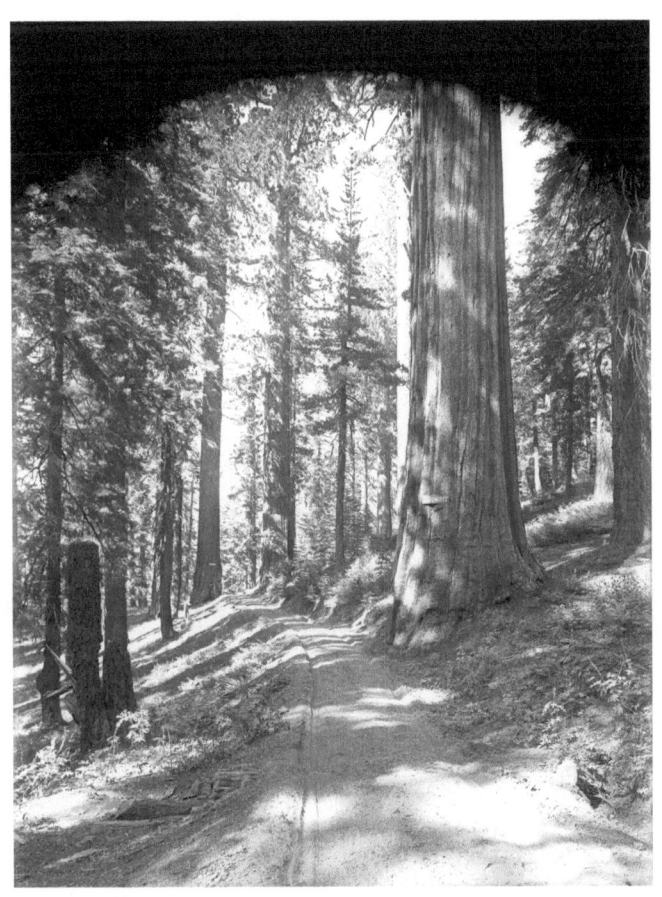

Vermont Tree, Road Study (1557, 6.5" x 8.5")

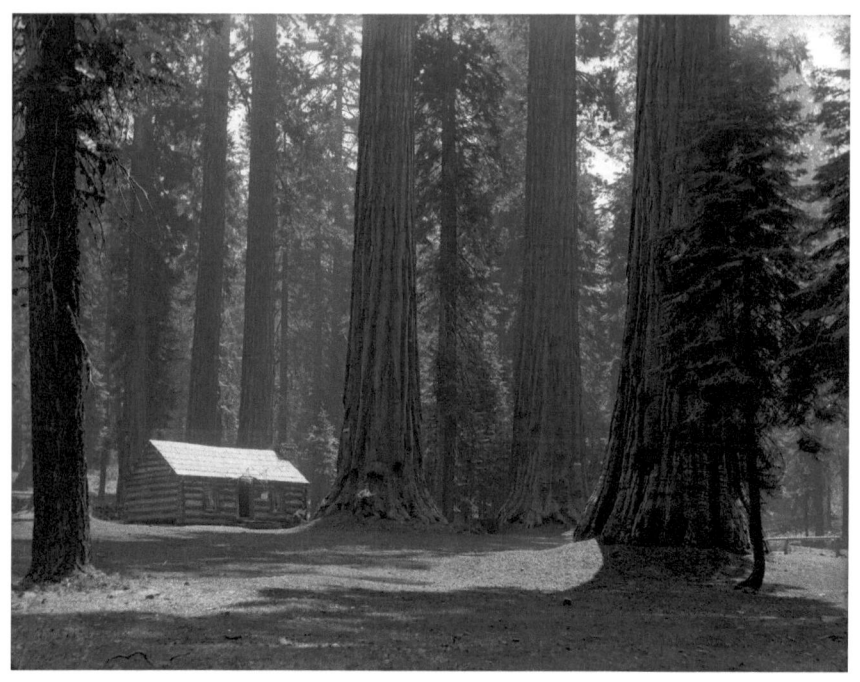

Old Cabin in Grove (1515, 6.5" x 8.5")

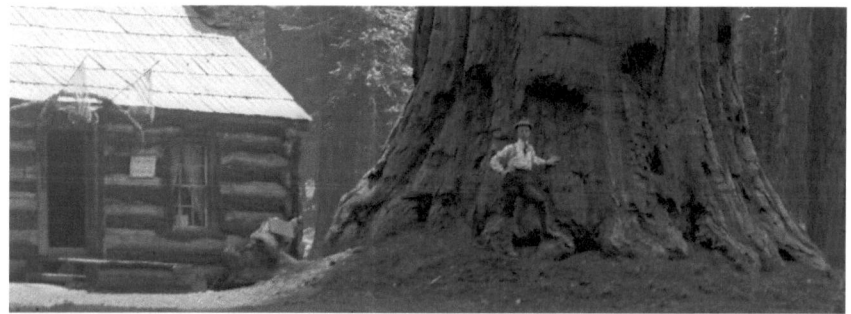

Detail of *Old Cabin in Grove* (1515, 6.5" x 8.5")

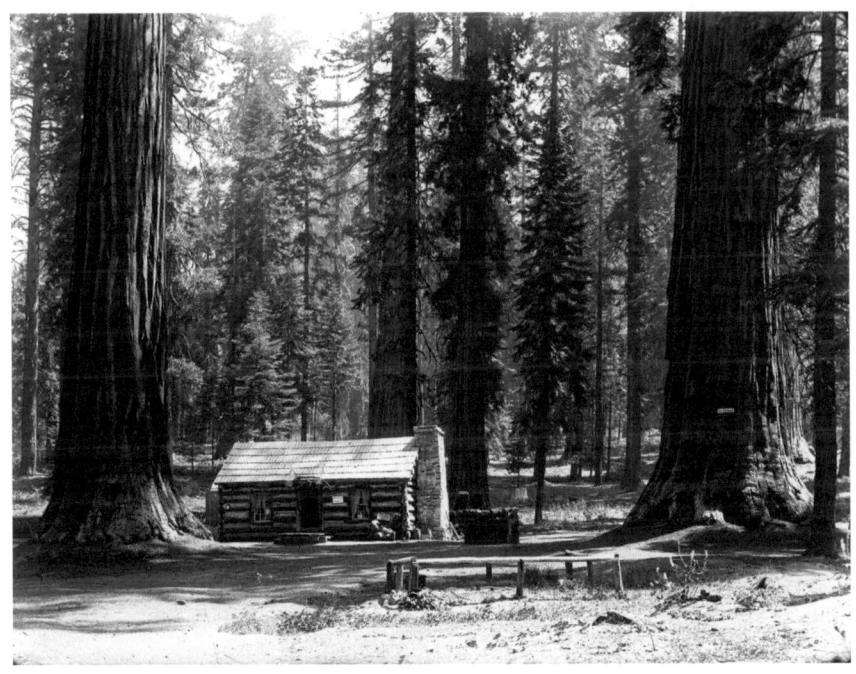

Old Cabin in Grove (1522b, 6.5" x 8.5")

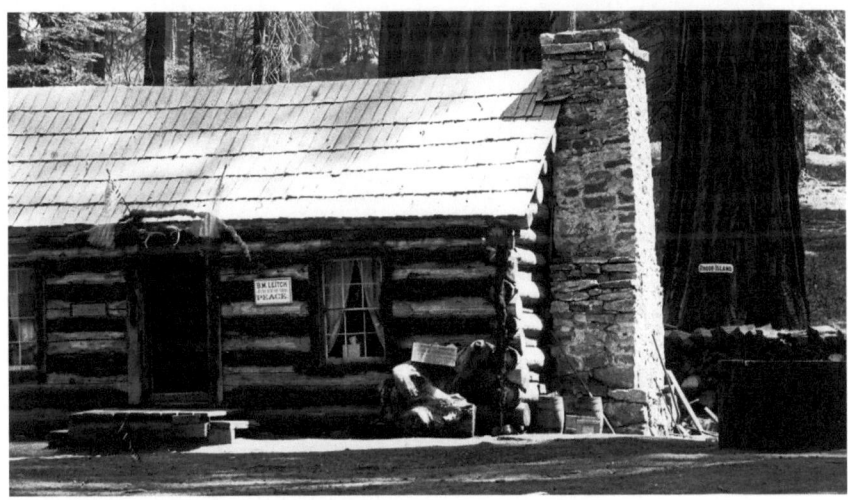

Detail of *Old Cabin in Grove* (1522b, 6.5" x 8.5")
Sign on cabin reads: "B.M. Leitch Justice of the Peace." Rhode Island Tree behind.

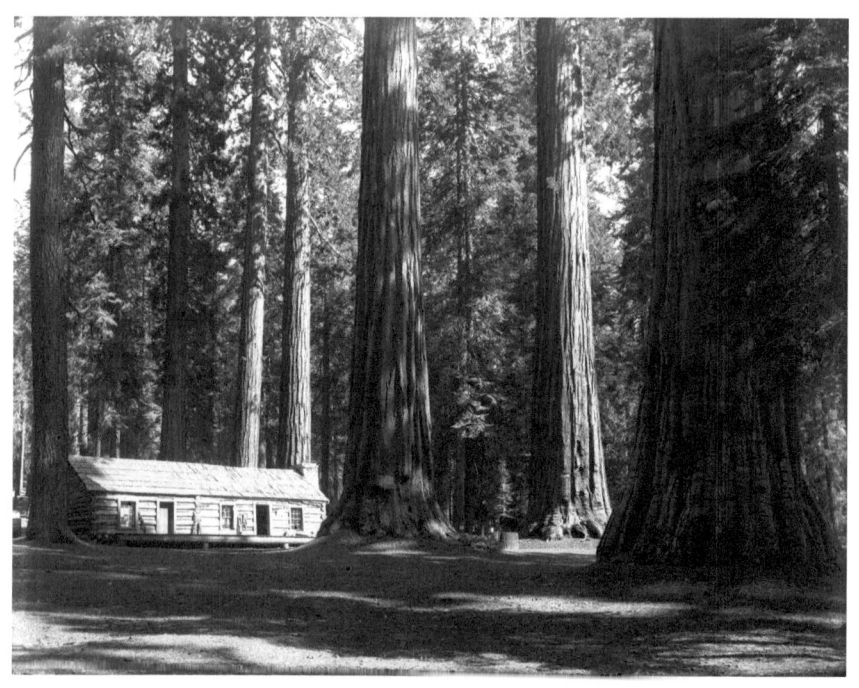

Cabin in Grove (1522a, 6.5" x 8.5")

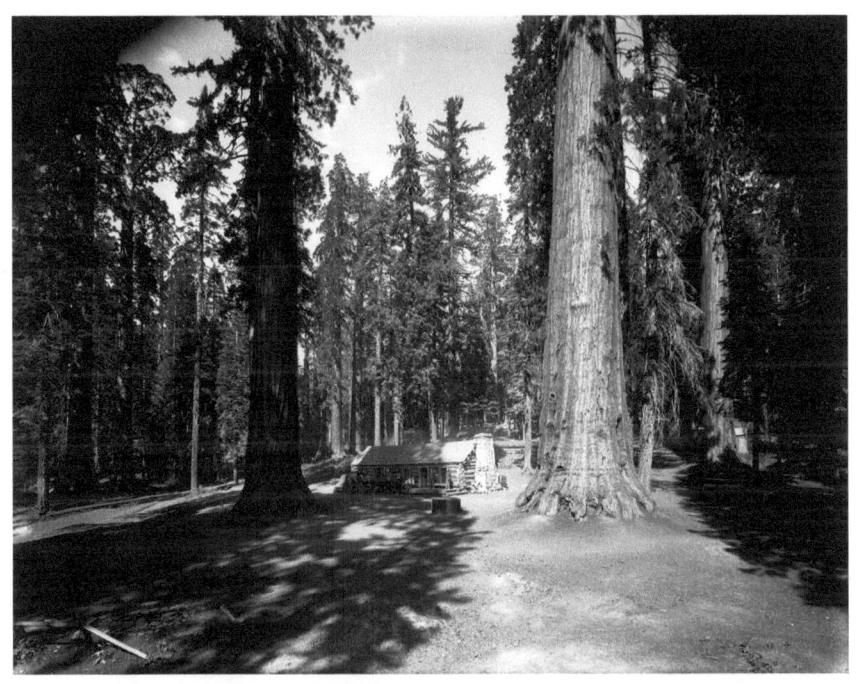

Cabin in Grove with Carriage (1542, 6.5" x 8.5")

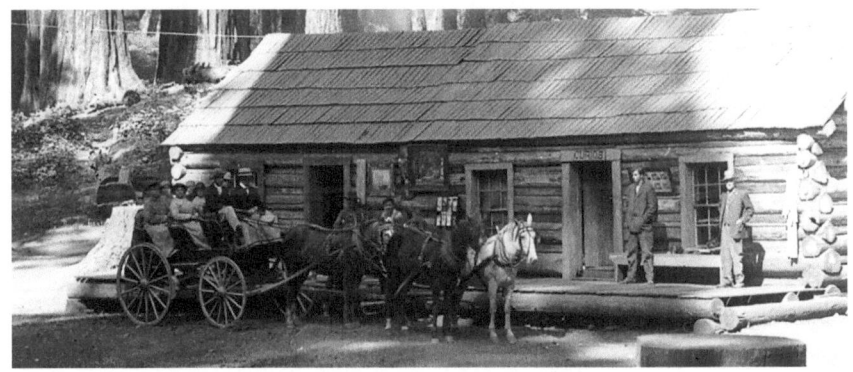

Detail of *Cabin in Grove with Carriage* (1542, 6.5" x 8.5")

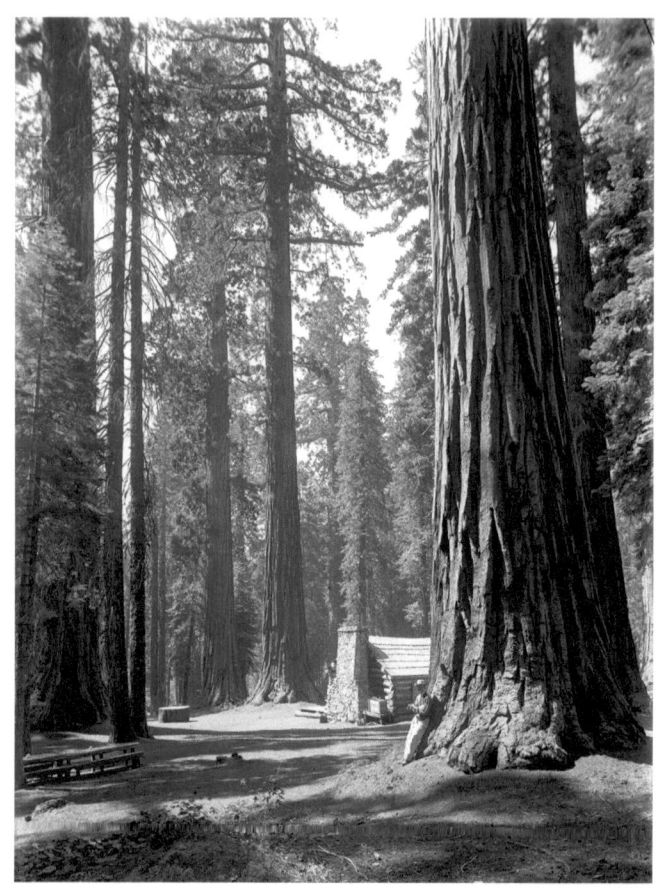

Cabin in Grove with Man (1543, 6.5" x 8.5")

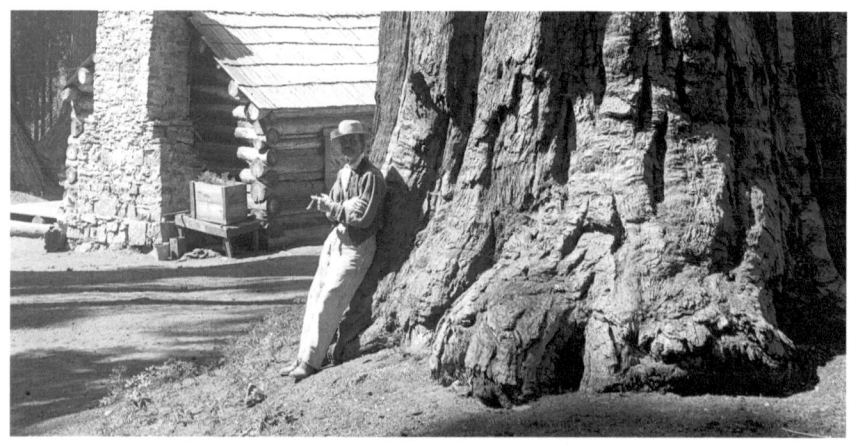

Detail of *Cabin in Grove with Man* (1543, 6.5" x 8.5")

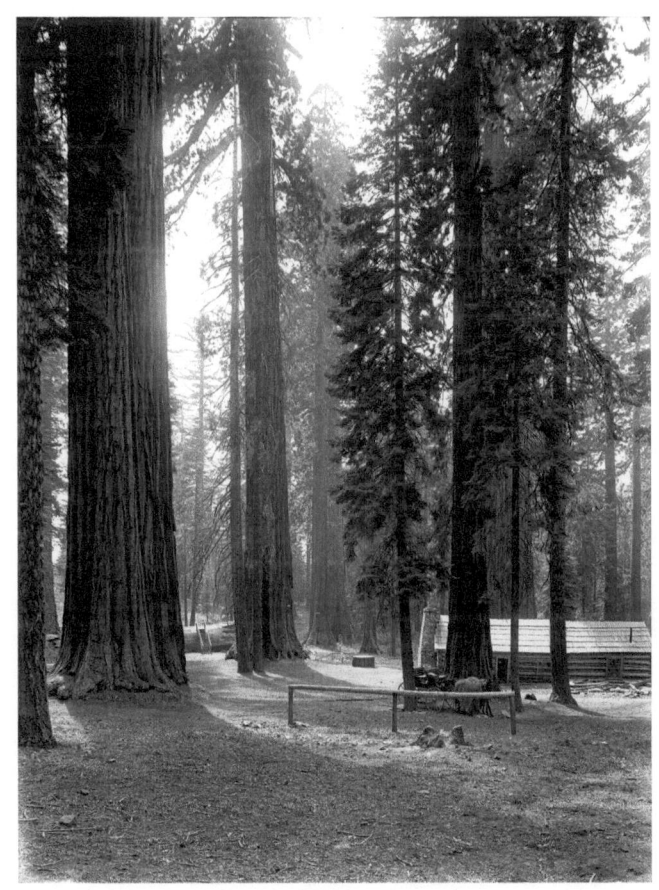

Cabin in Grove, Fallen Tree with Stairs (1541, 6.5" x 8.5")

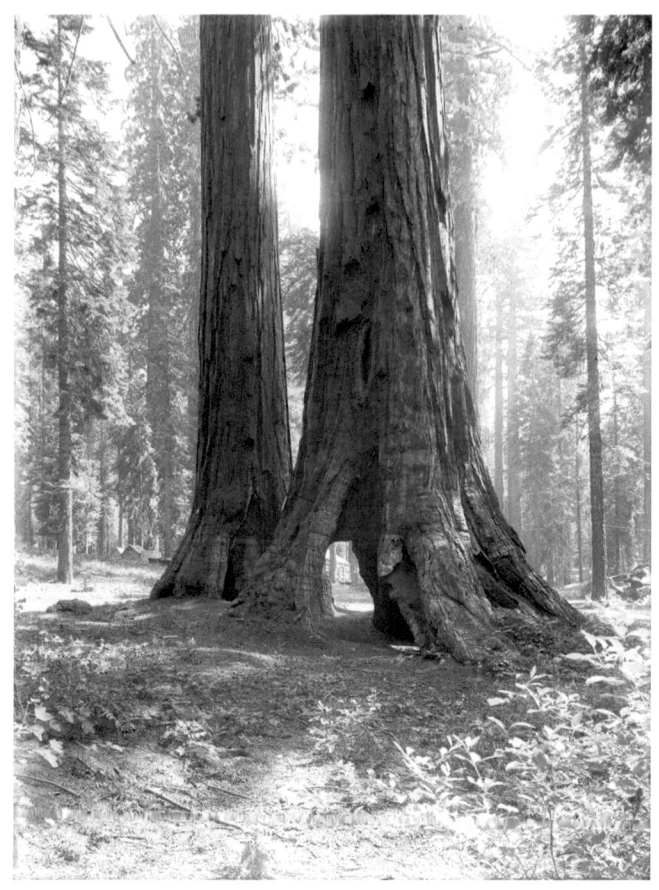

Haverford and Ohio Trees with View of Cabins (1539, 6.5" x 8.5")

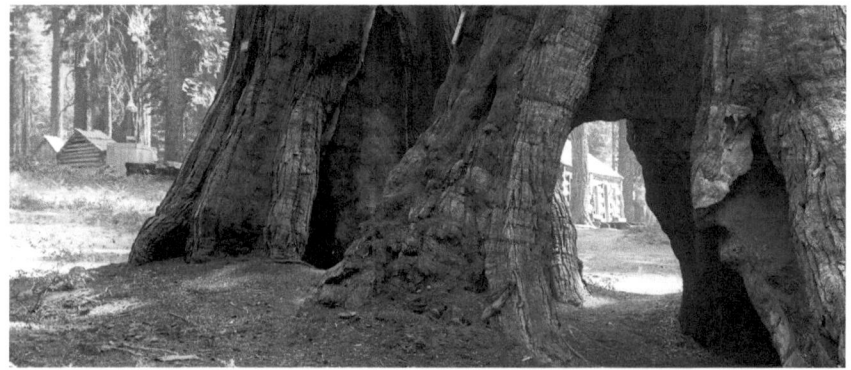

Detail of *Haverford and Ohio Trees with View of Cabins* (1539, 6.5" x 8.5")

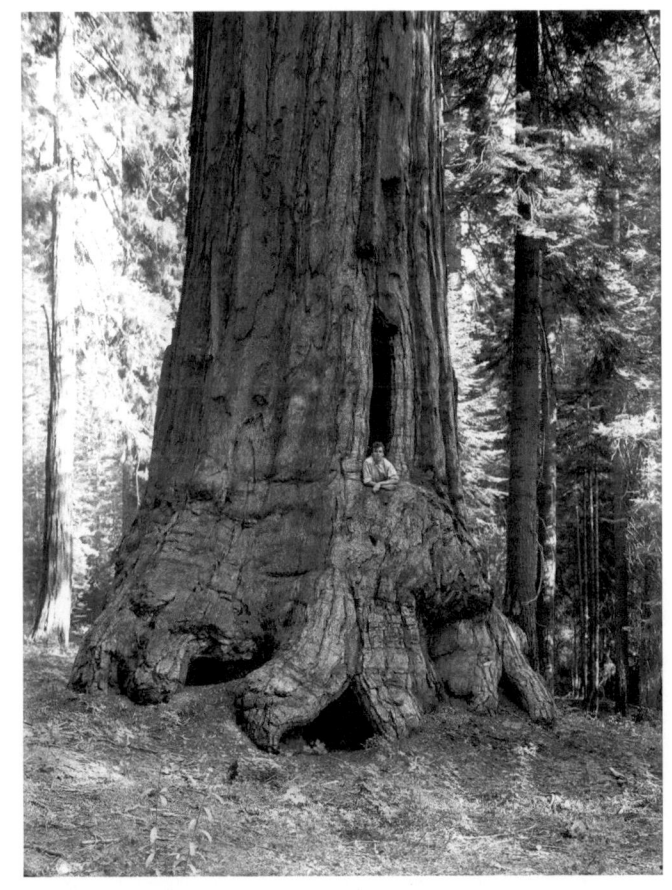

Governor Tree with Man (1536, 6.5" x 8.5")

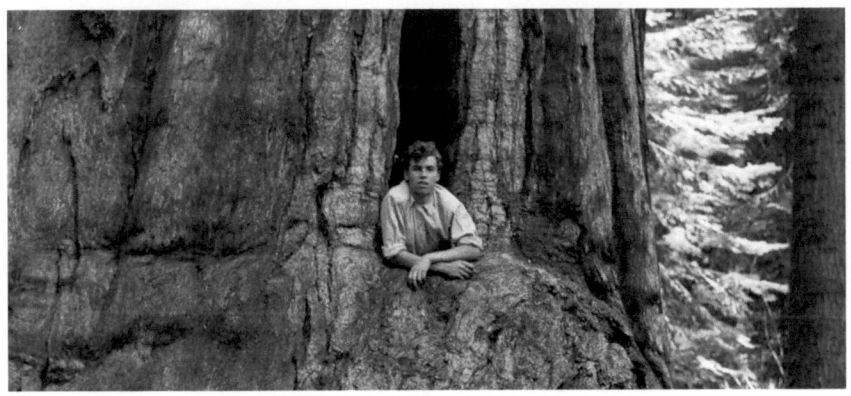

Detail of *Governor Tree with Man* (1536, 6.5" x 8.5")

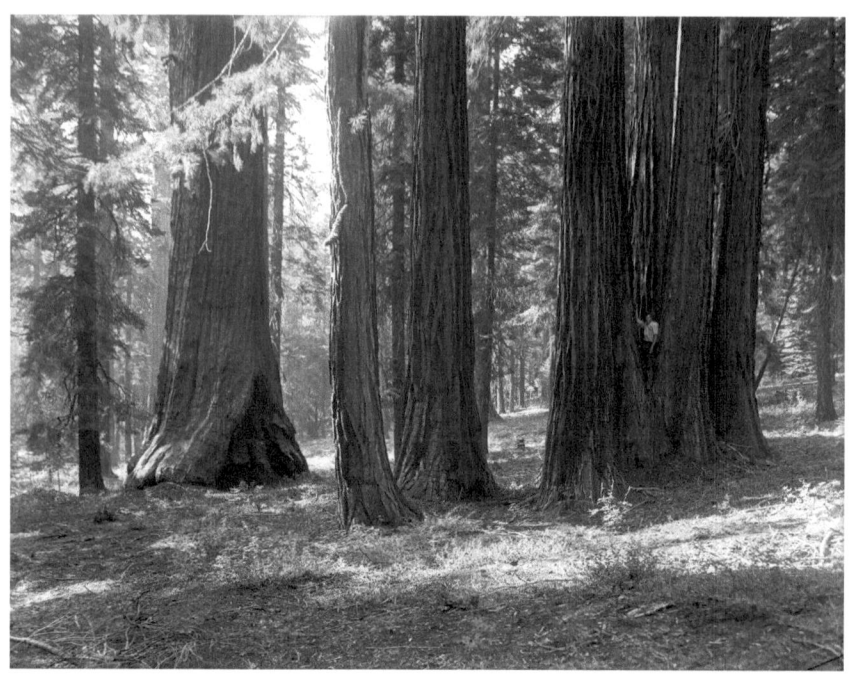

Governor and Commissioners Trees with Man (1538, 6.5" x 8.5")

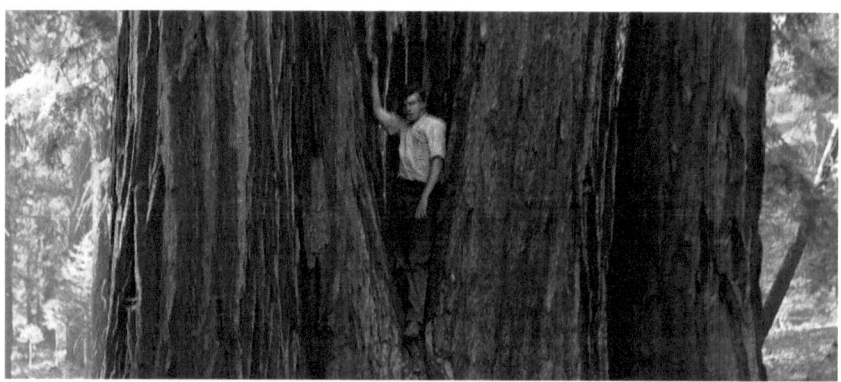

Detail of *Governor and Commissioners Trees with Man* (1538, 6.5" x 8.5")

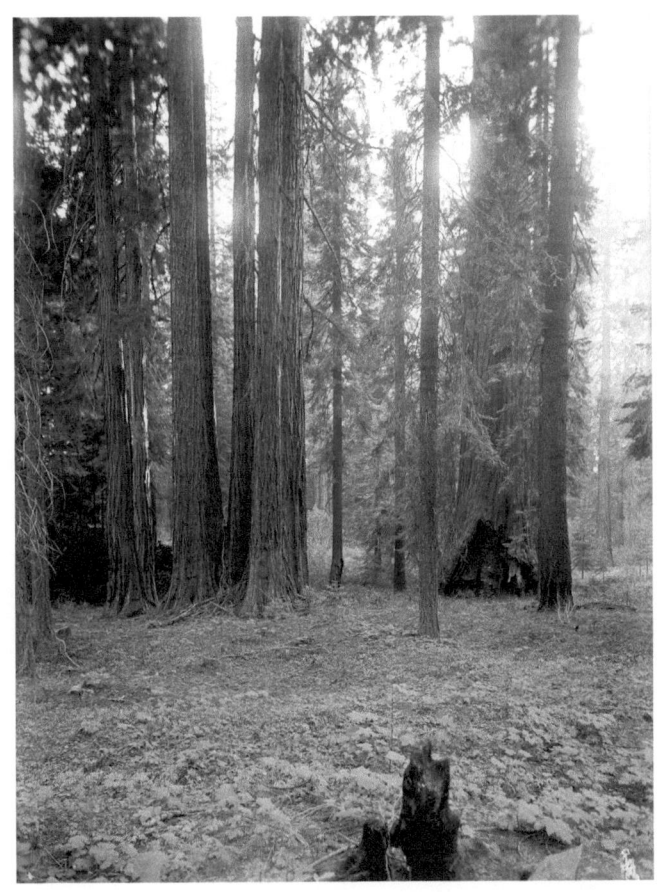
Governor and Commissioners Trees (1537, 6.5" x 8.5")

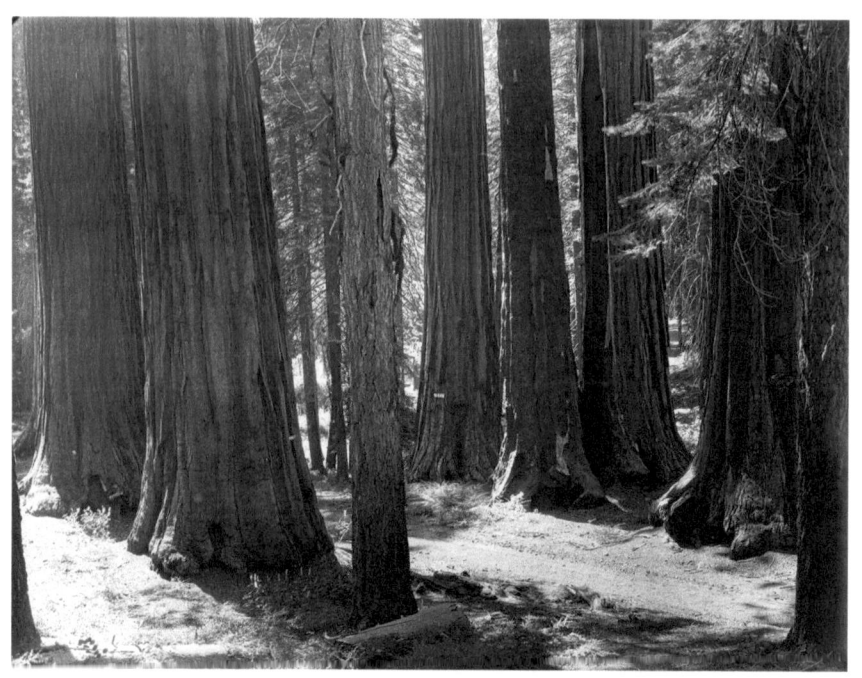

Governor Gene Todd Group (1524b, 6.5" x 8.5")

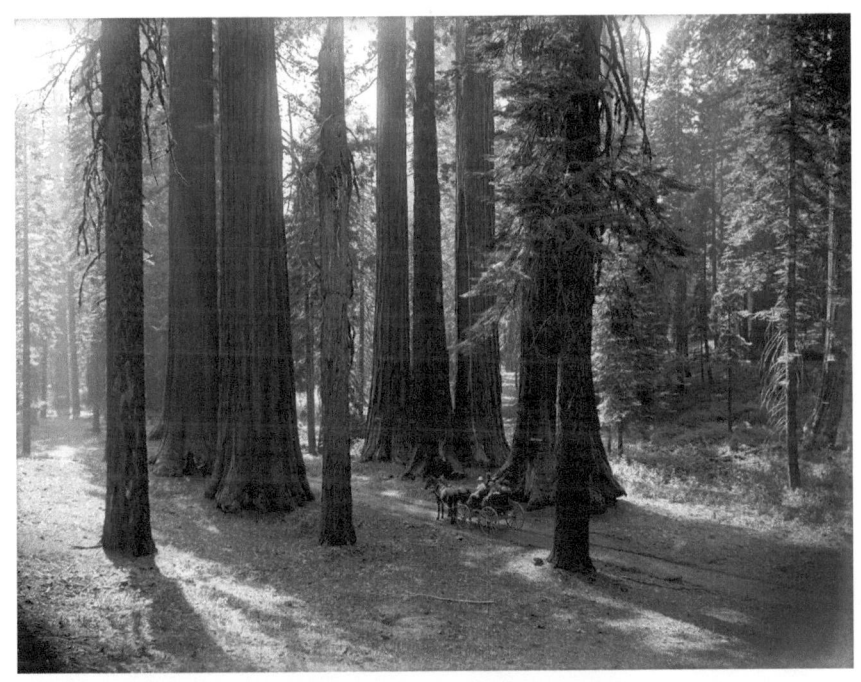

Governor Gene Todd Group with Carriage (1547, 6.5" x 8.5")

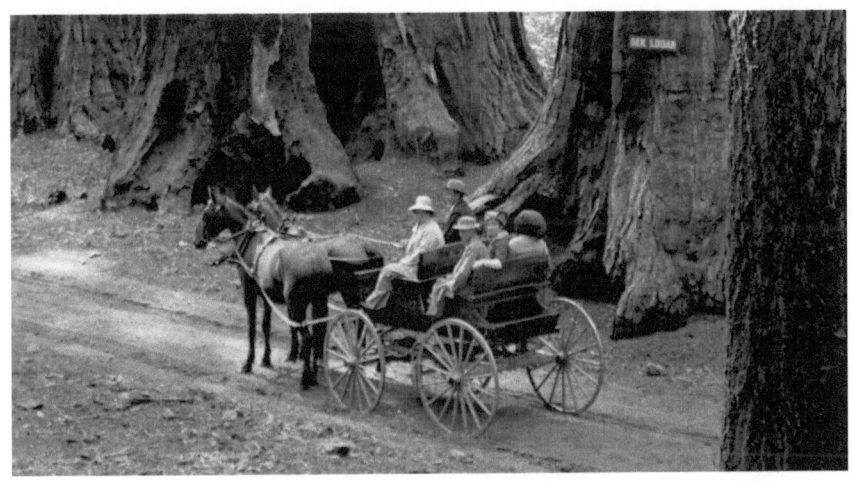

Detail of *Governor Gene Todd Group with Carriage* (1547, 6.5" x 8.5")

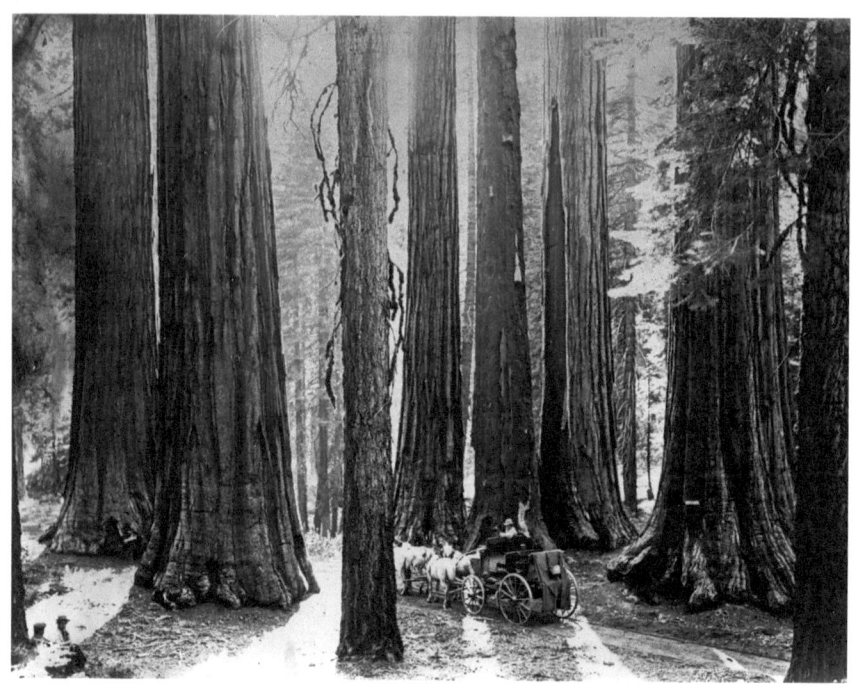

Governor Gene Todd Group with Carriage (1524a, 6.5" x 8.5")

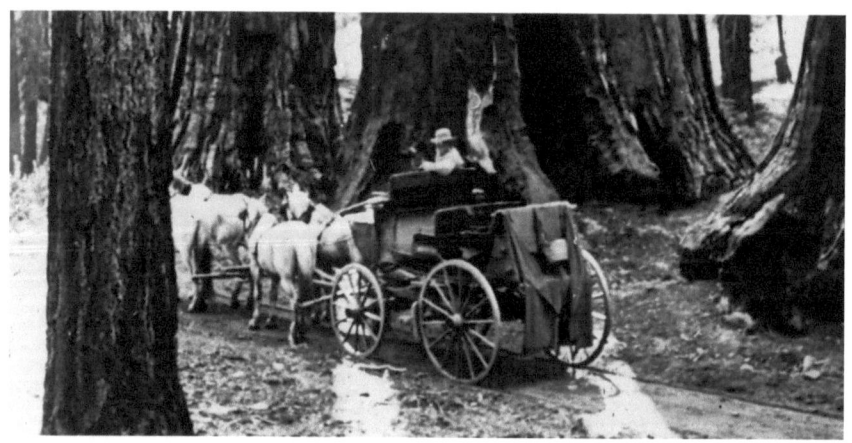

Detail of *Governor Gene Todd Group with Carriage* (1524a, 6.5" x 8.5")

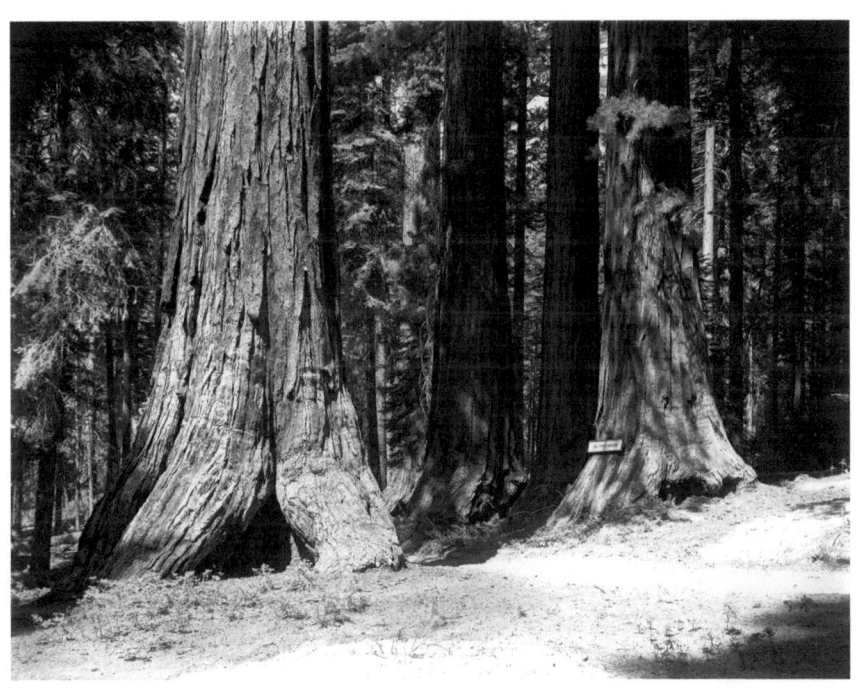

Bachelor and Three Graces (1527, 6.5" x 8.5")

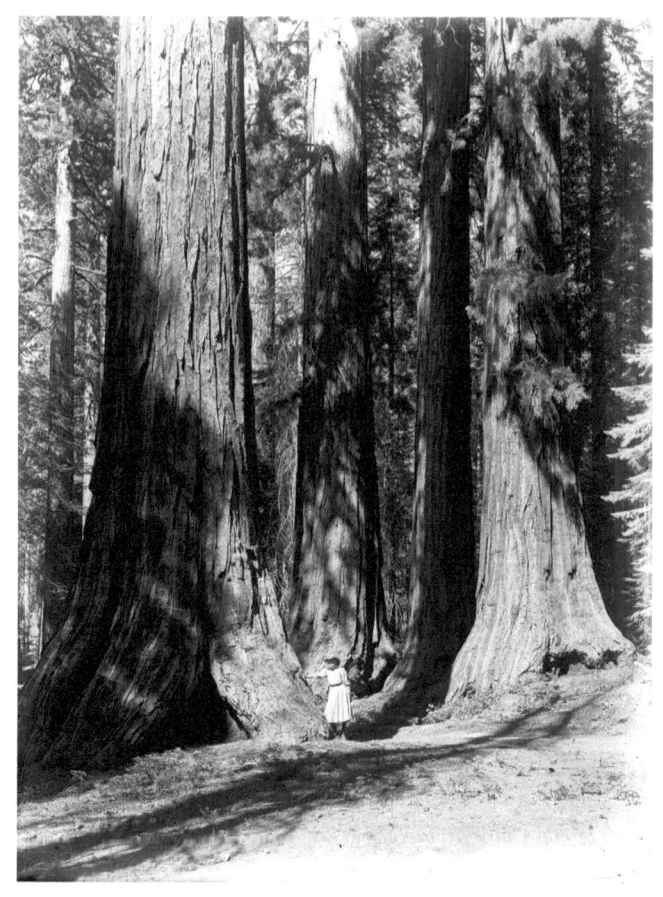

Bachelor and Three Graces with Lady (1505, 6.5" x 8.5")

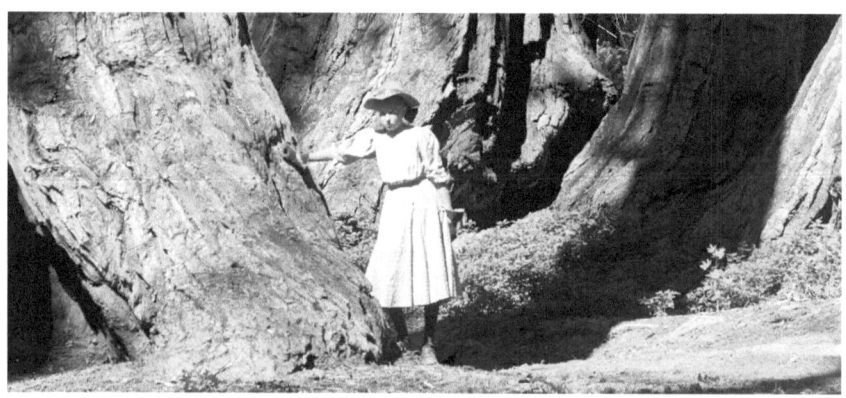

Detail of *Bachelor and Three Graces with Lady* (1505, 6.5" x 8.5")

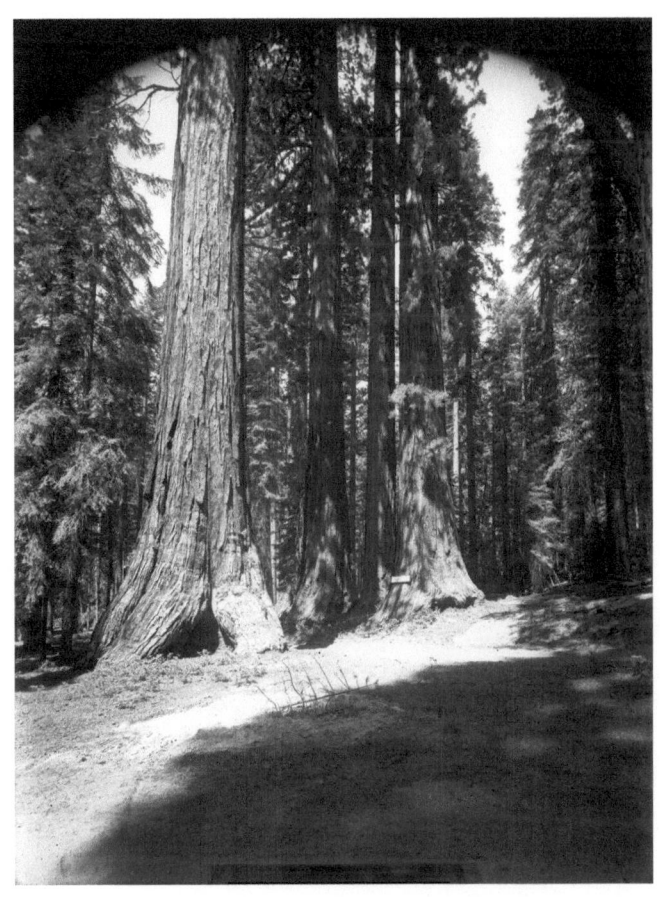

Bachelor and Three Graces (1528, 6.5" x 8.5")

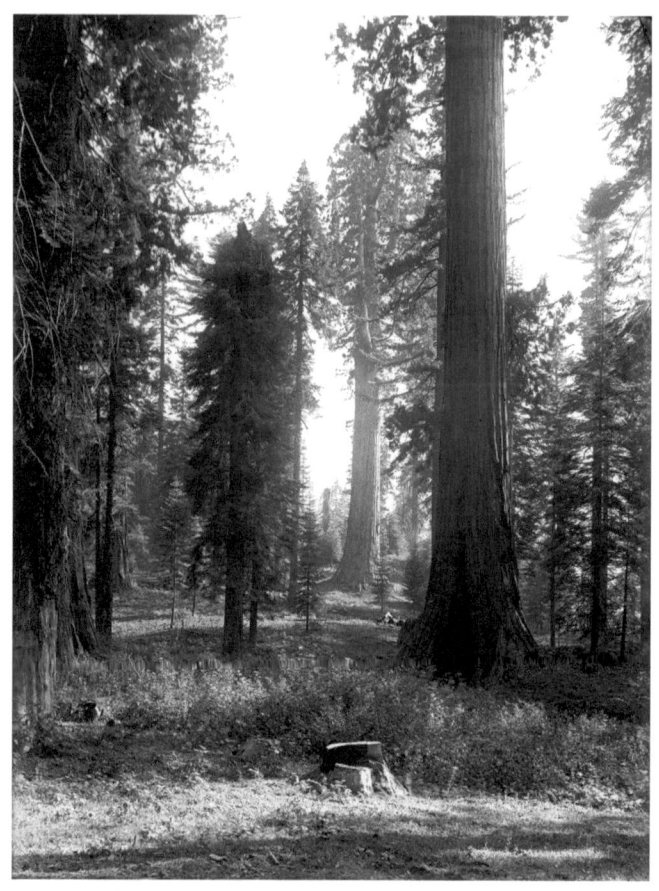

Confederate Group and Telescope Tree (1552, 6.5" x 8.5")

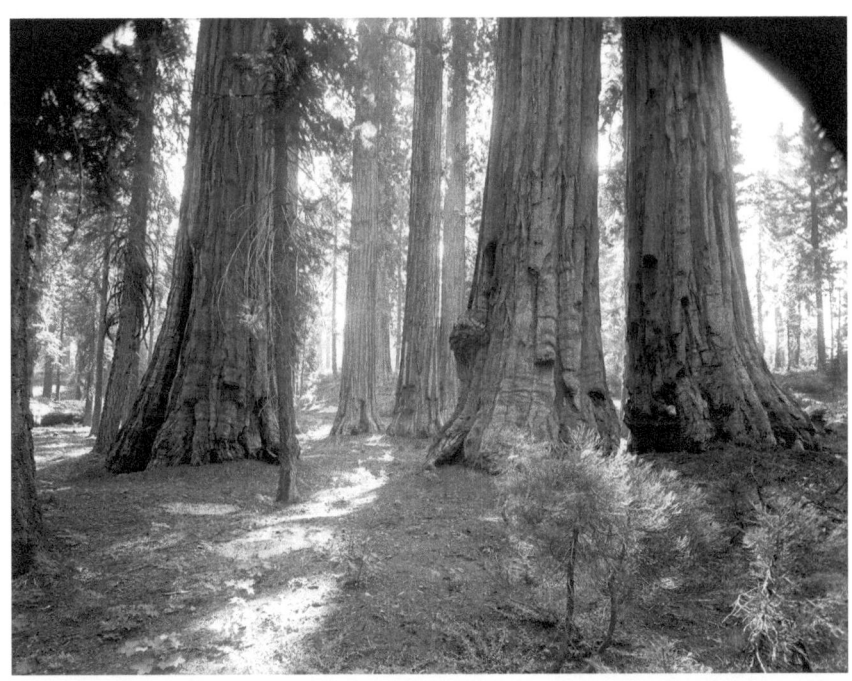

Confederate Group, Rear View (1551, 6.5" x 8.5")

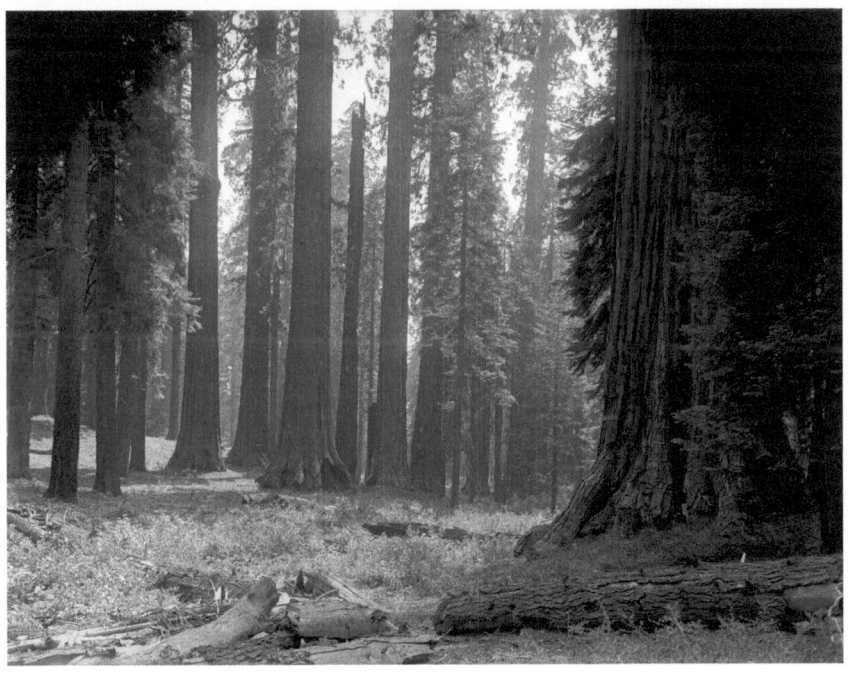

William McKinley Group (1548, 6.5" x 8.5")

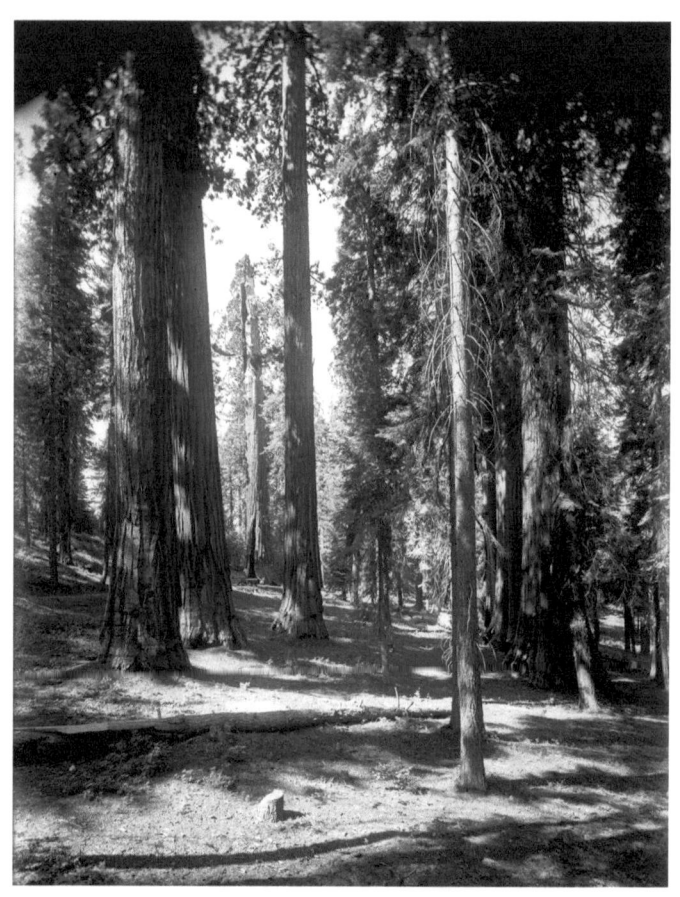
Columbia and Massachusetts (1546, 6.5" x 8.5")

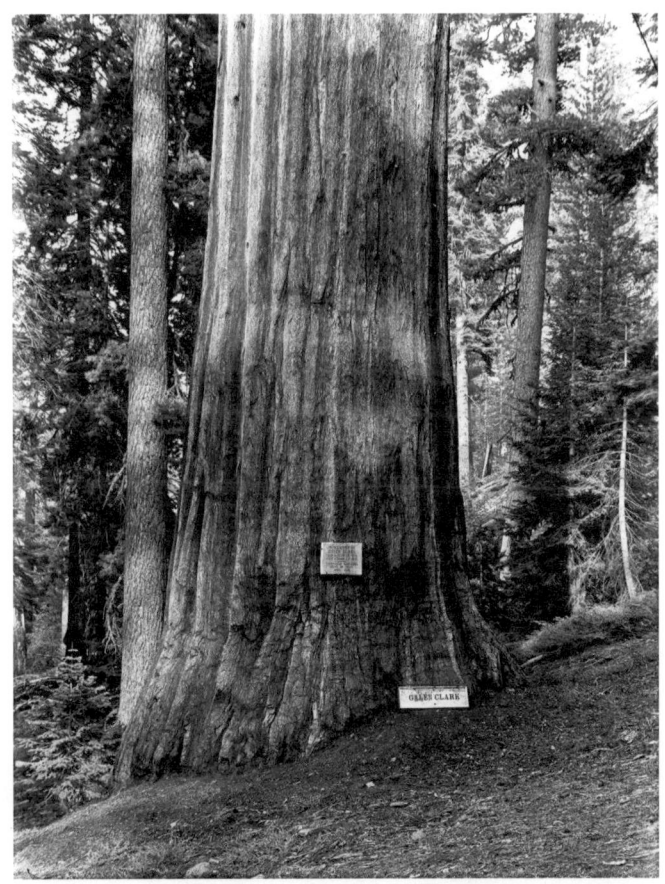

Galen Clark (1559, 6.5" x 8.5")

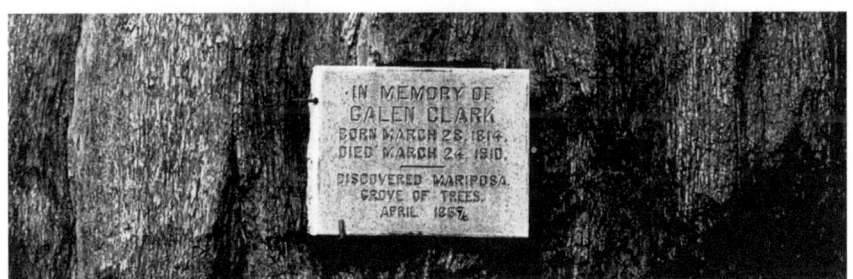

Detail of *Galen Clark* (1559, 6.5" x 8.5")

"In Memory of Galen Clark / Born March 28, 1814 / Died March 24, 1910 / Discovered Mariposa Grove of Trees April 1857"

This image shows that Harold Taylor visited the Sequoias after his 1902-1907 tenure in Yosemite Valley since the plaque postdates Galen Clark's death in 1910.

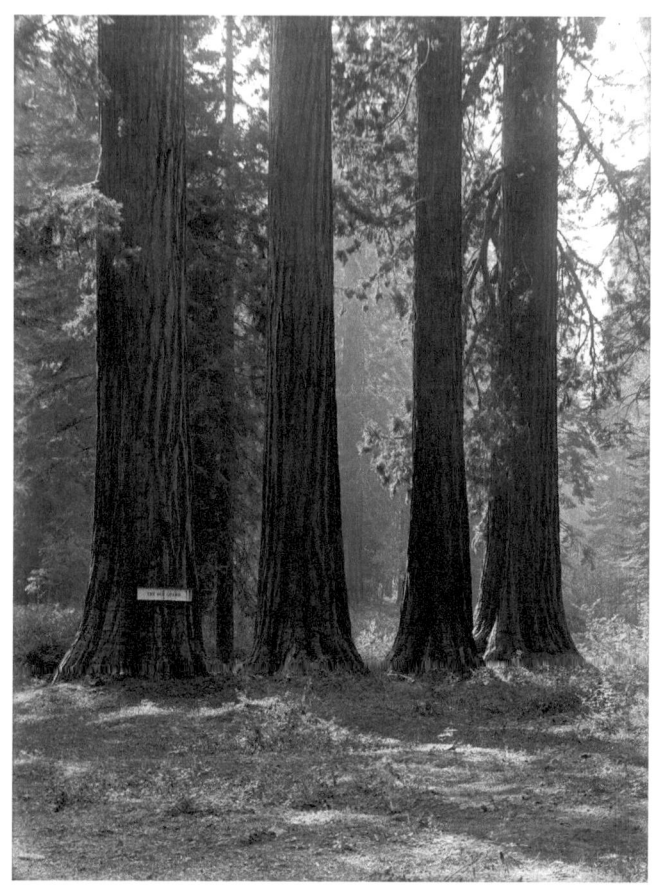

The Old Guard (1545, 6.5" x 8.5")

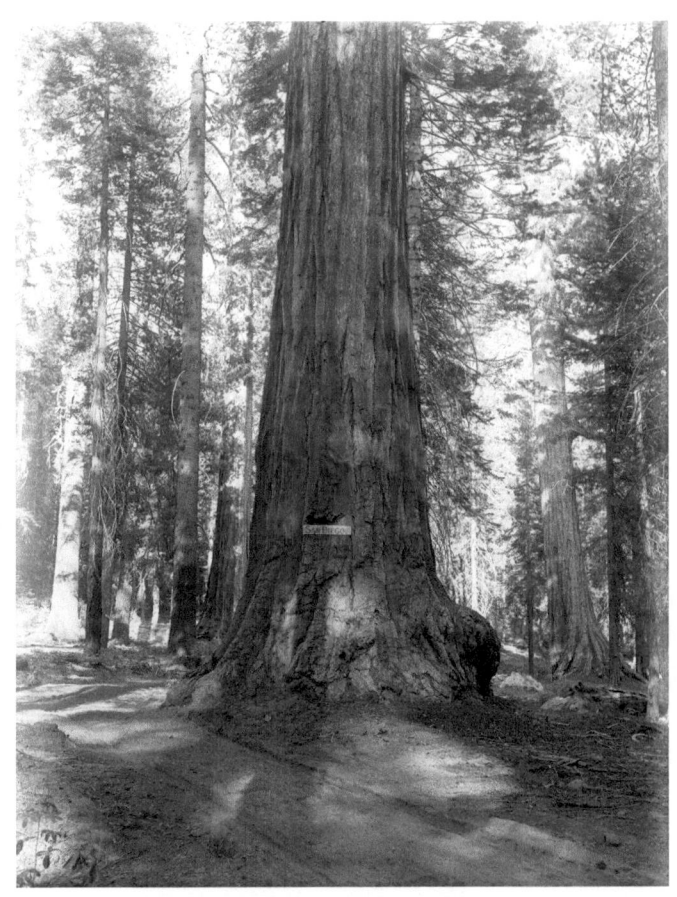

San Diego (1517, 6.5" x 8.5")

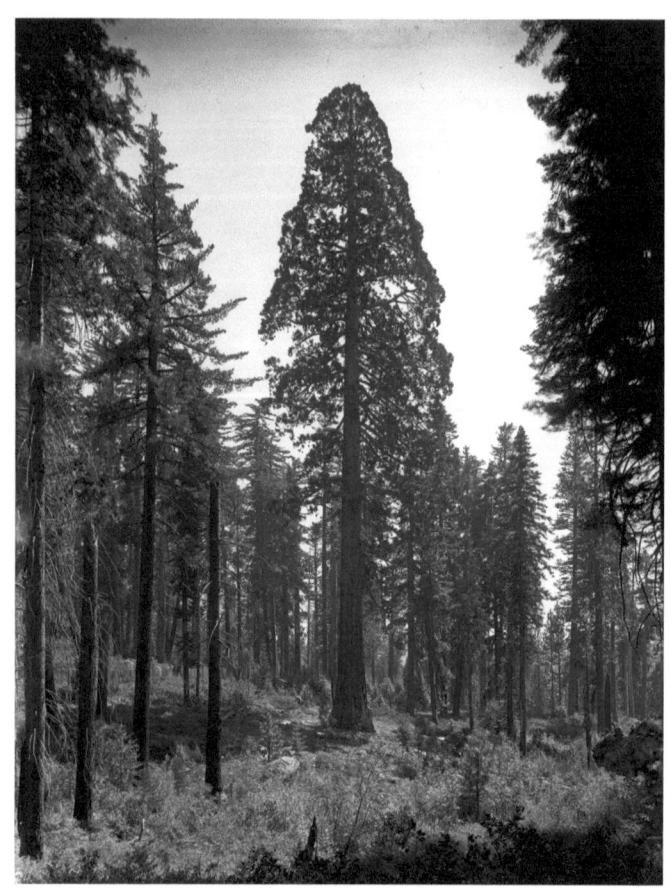

Most Perfect Tree, Alabama (1534, 6.5" x 8.5")

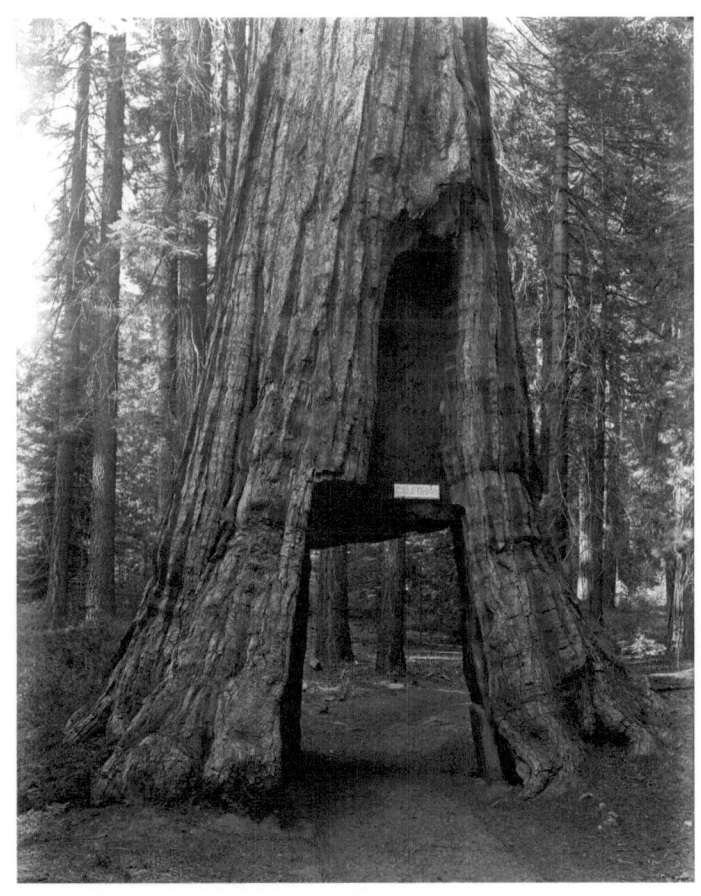

California (1506, 6.5" x 8.5")

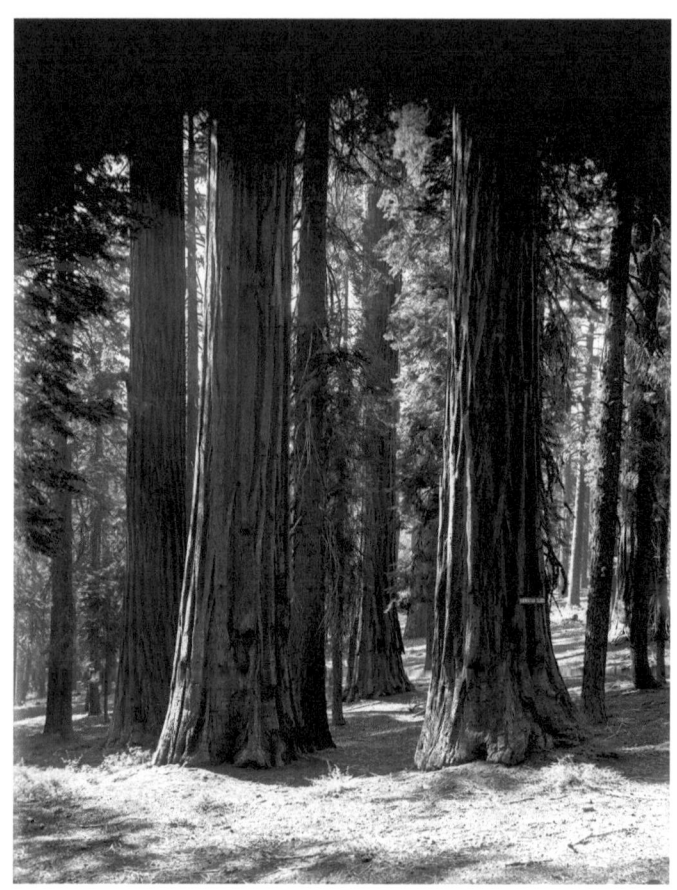

Hawaiian Islands (1558, 6.5" x 8.5")

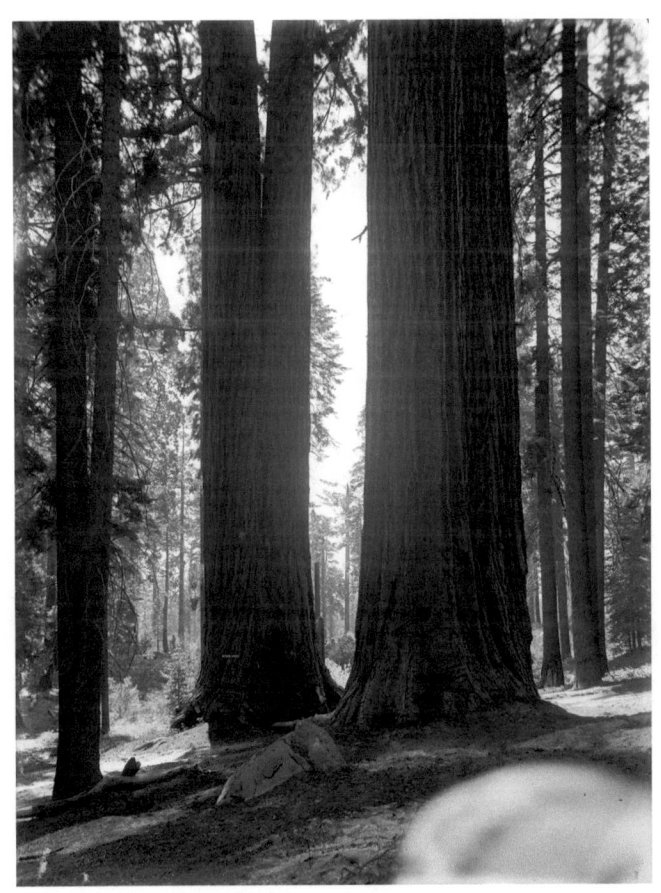

Faithful Couple (1533, 6.5" x 8.5")

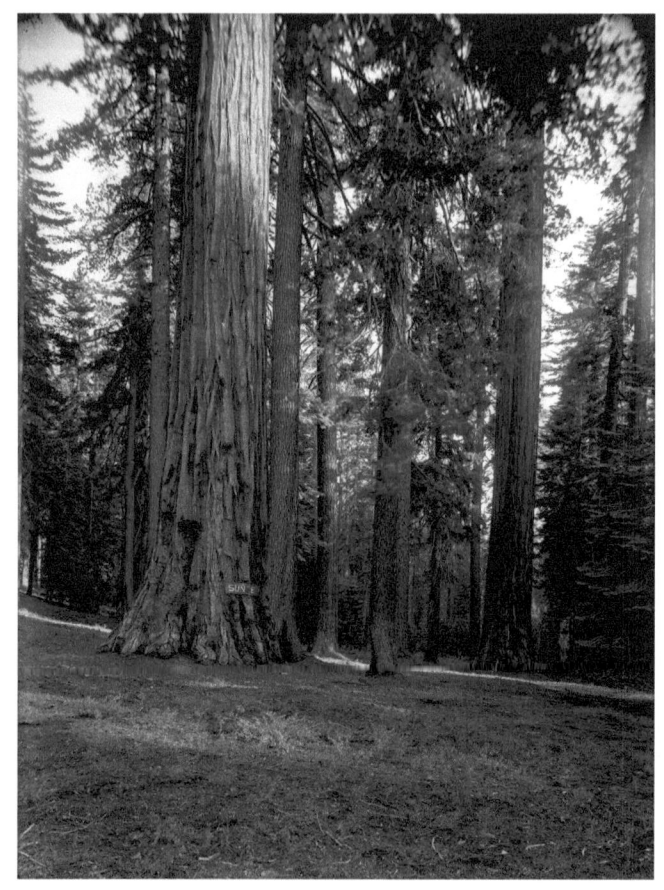

Sunset Tree (1535, 6.5" x 8.5")

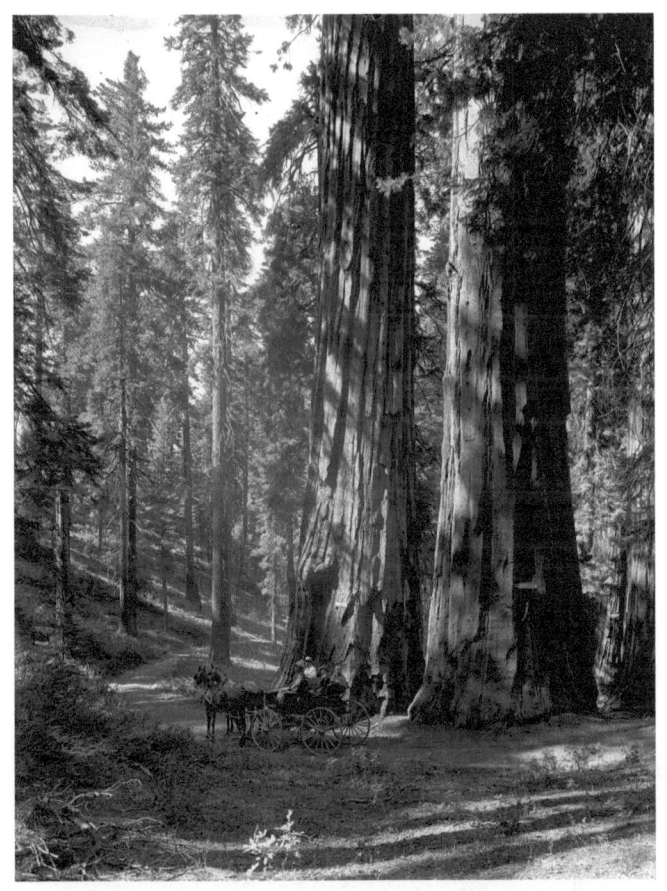

Longfellow and Whittier with Carriage (1553, 6.5" x 8.5")

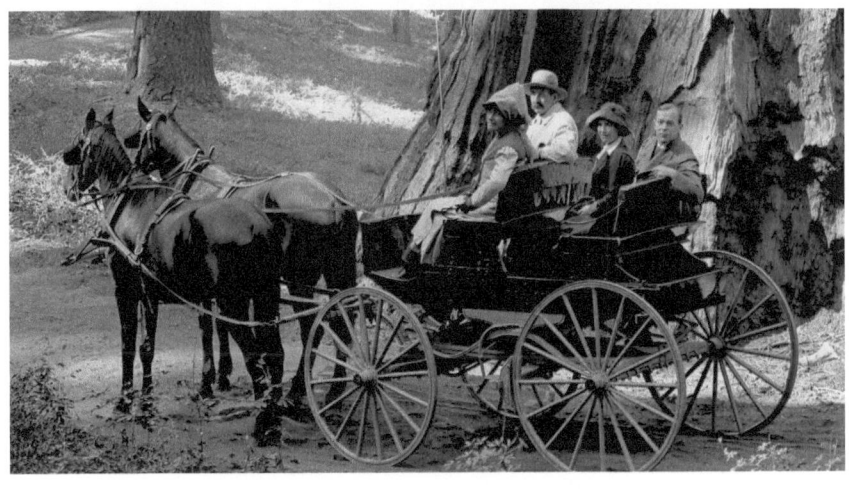

Detail of *Longfellow and Whittier with Carriage* (1553, 6.5" x 8.5")

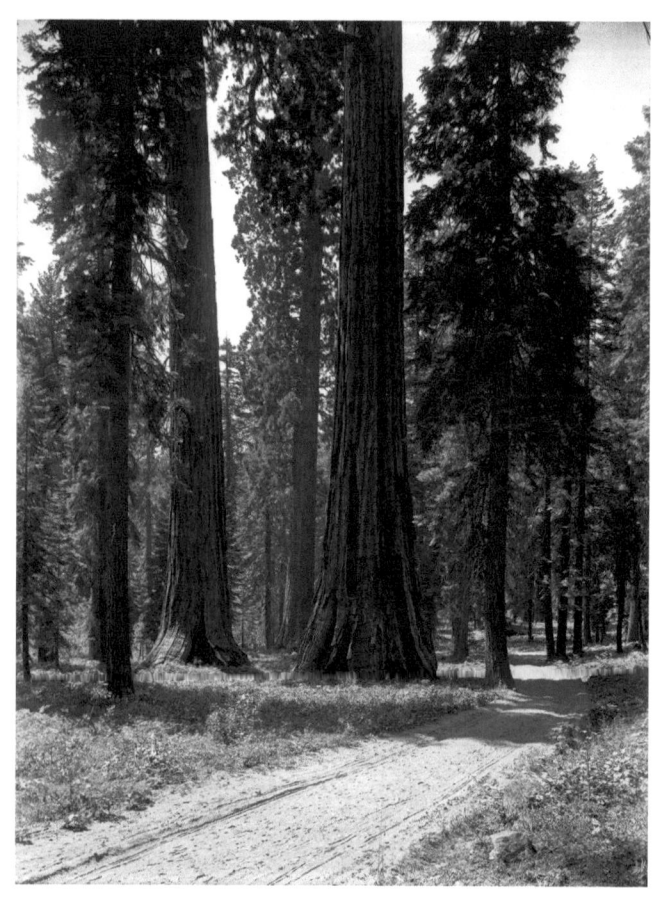

Sequoia Road Study (1549, 6.5" x 8.5")

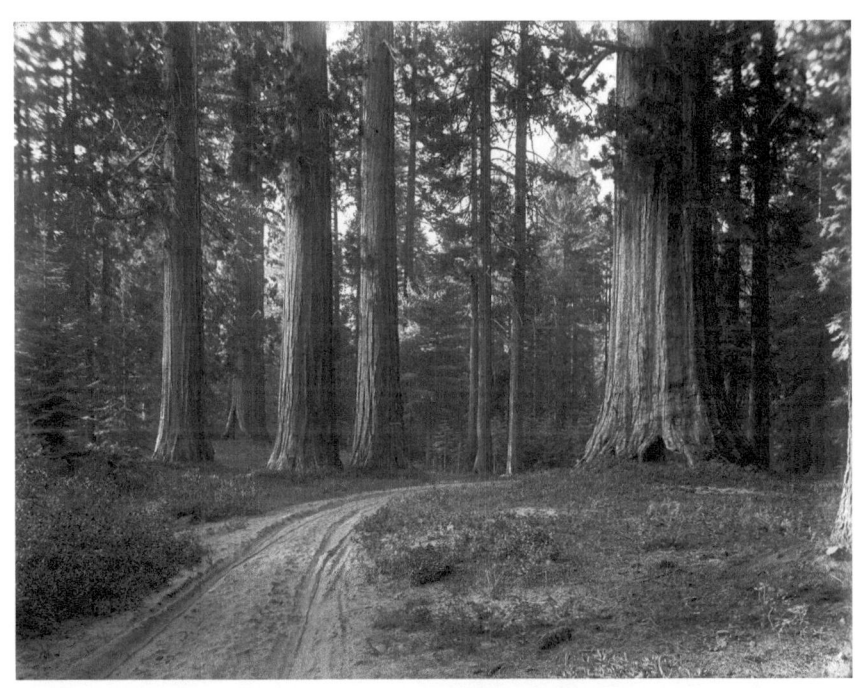

Sequoia Road Study, Diamond Group (1560, 6.5" x 8.5")

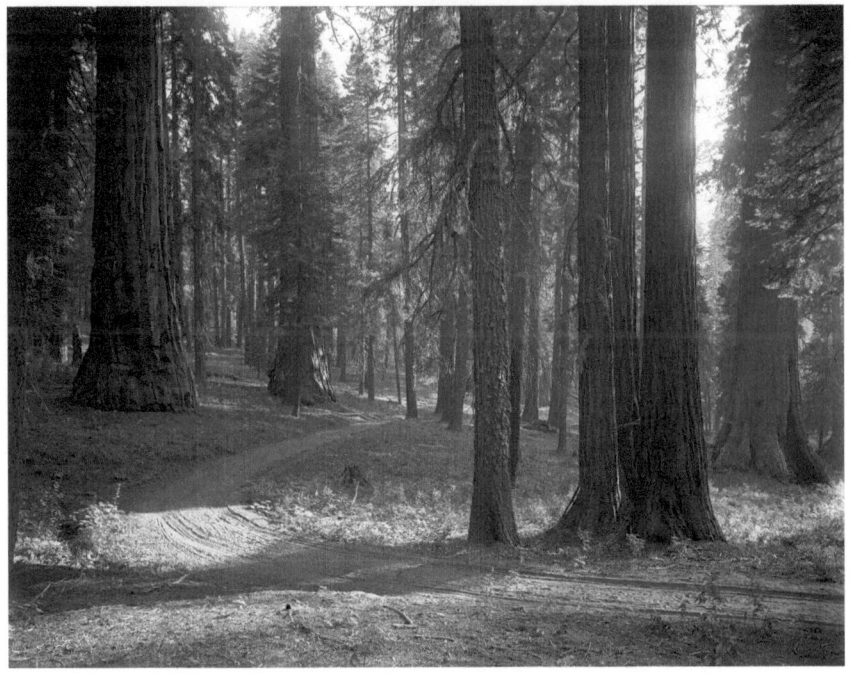

Sequoia Road Study (1550, 6.5" x 8.5")

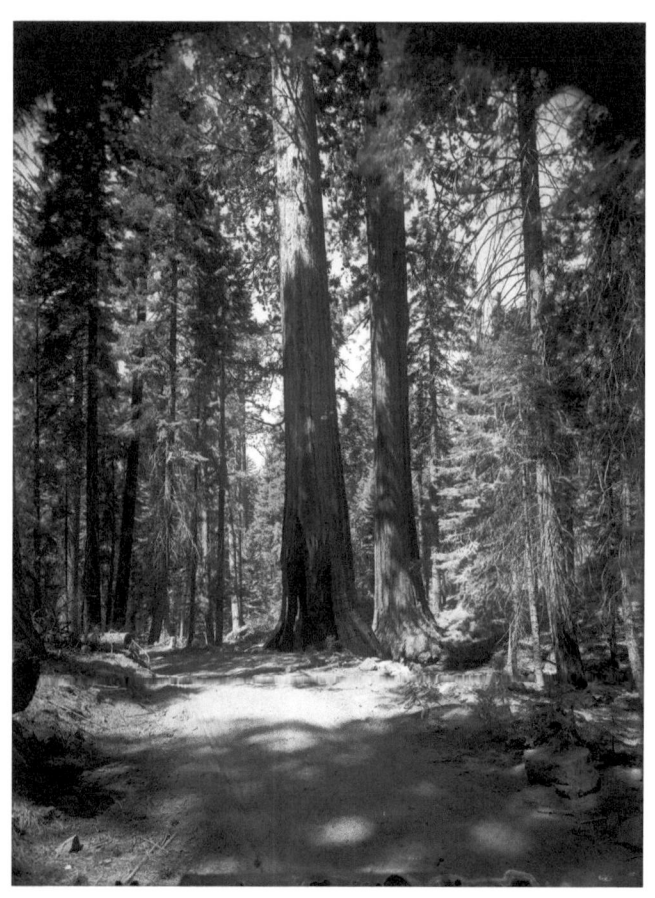
Lower Grove Road (1529, 6.5" x 8.5")

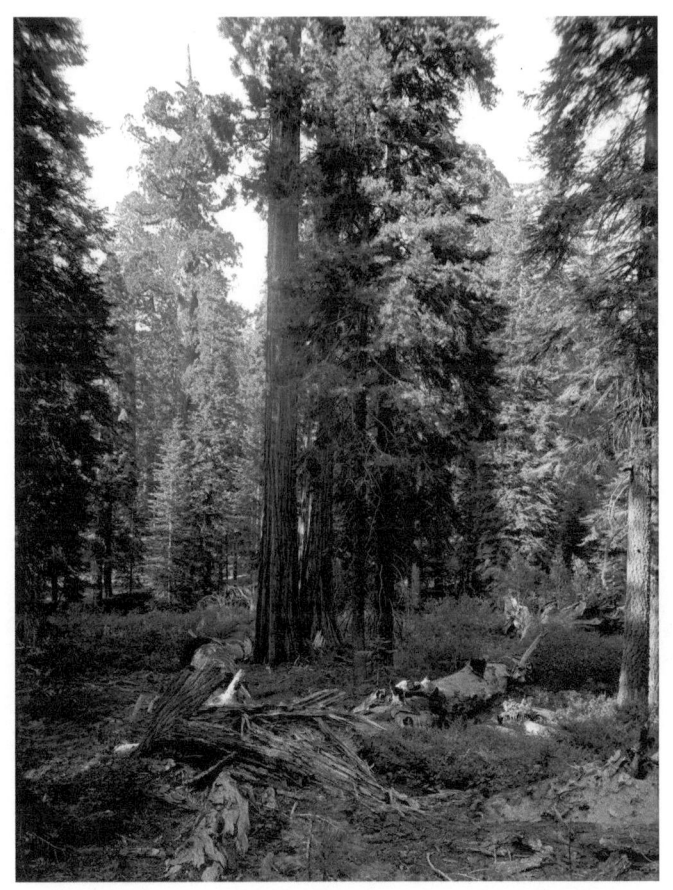
Dead and Living Among the Big Trees (1544, 6.5" x 8.5")

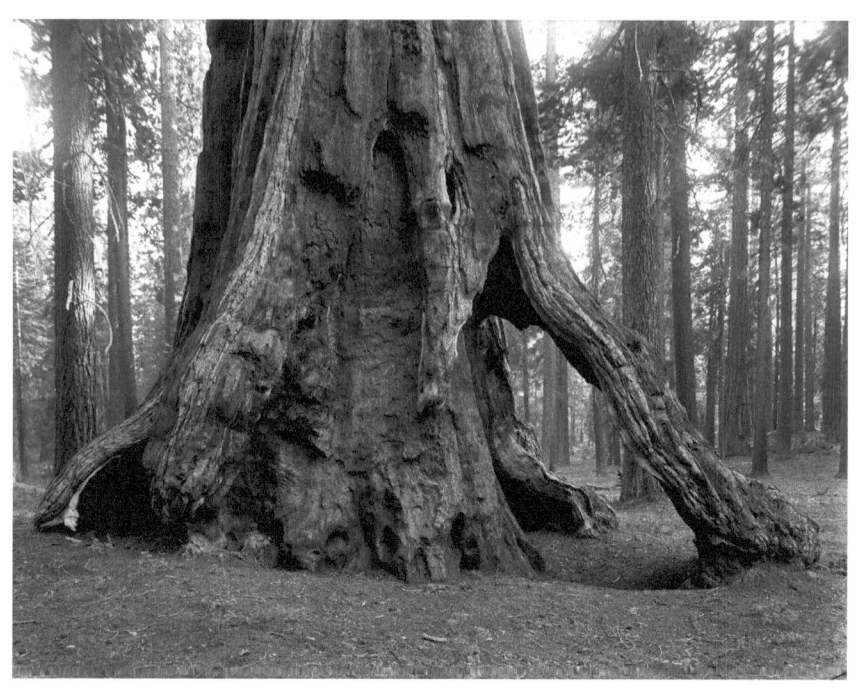

The Base of a Sequoia (1540, 6.5" x 8.5")

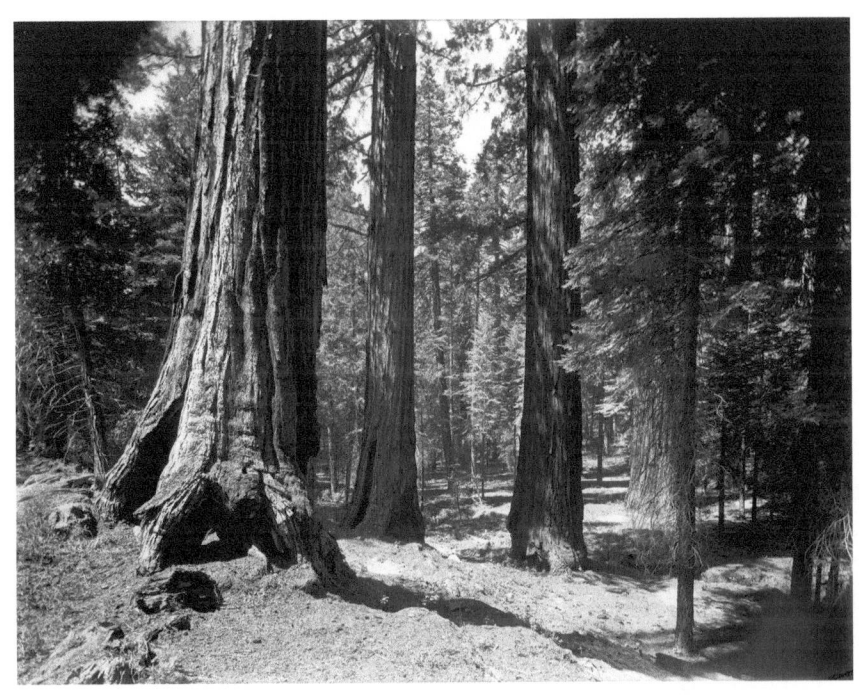

Among Giants (1526, 6.5" x 8.5")

PRESERVING GLASS PLATE NEGATIVES

In the early 1870s Richard Leach Maddox (English photographer and physician) invented the dry gelatin glass plate negative. While using the photographic precursor (wet collodion glass plates) for microphotography of minute organisms, Maddox had noticed ill effects of the vapor from the ether used in the process. The dangerous chemicals had to be applied to the glass plate just before exposure and then developed in a darkroom within minutes before it dried. Maddox's new dry glass plates were coated ahead of time with light-sensitive silver nitrate dissolved in gelatin. Dry glass plate negatives were safer, easier to use outside, and produced sharper images. They dominated photography until the more convenient flexible celluloid roll film took over in the late 1920s.

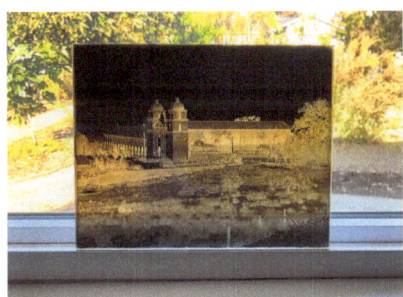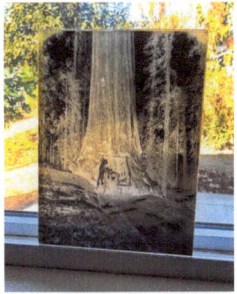

Glass Plate Negatives of *Santa Barbara Mission* & *Wawona Tree with Coach*

The Elliott collection of Harold A. Taylor's glass plates includes 153 plates of Yosemite National Park, 144 plates of California missions, and 27 miscellaneous plates. The fragile 100-year-old plates are mostly 5" x 7", 6.5" x 8.5", or 8" x 10" and are about 1/16" thick.

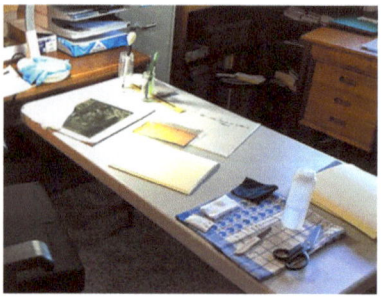 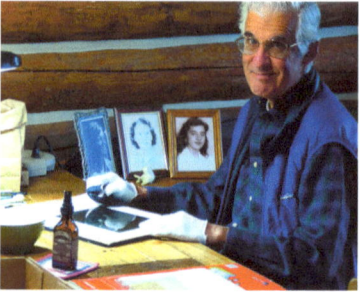

Robert Elliott, Cleaning Glass Plate Negatives

For many decades, Harold Taylor's glass plates were hiding away in paper sleeves with his (or his assistant's) lovely penmanship noting their contents. We used a soft goat-hair brush and a thin blade to carefully remove any bits of paper that adhered to the plates. We avoided contact with the emulsion side since it is subject to flaking. But on the glossy non-emulsion side, we lightly removed dirt and polished the glass with cotton pads and distilled water. We transferred the cleaned plates to archival 4-fold sleeves which we store upright in archival boxes.

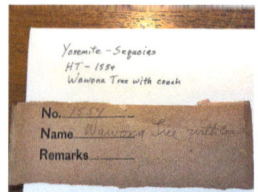 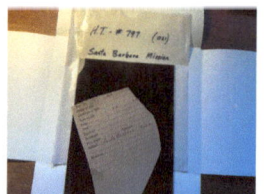 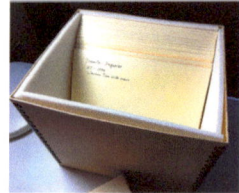

Glass Plate Negatives with Old and New Sleeves and Storage Box

We scanned each plate at high resolution with a scanner that allows light to pass through the plate. We then adjusted the digital images on the computer in a fashion akin to making developing adjustments in the darkroom. When desired, we digitally removed micro-scratches.

Of the 324 glass plates, 6 were cracked or broken in a way which required horizontal supported storage in a sink mat.

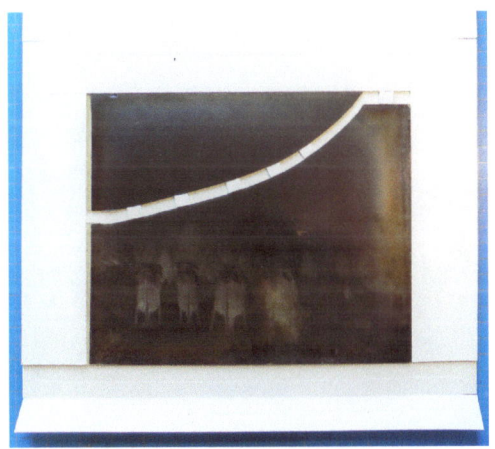

Indian Acorn Cache in a Sink Mat

The cracked plates still scanned well, and we also digitally removed some cracks.

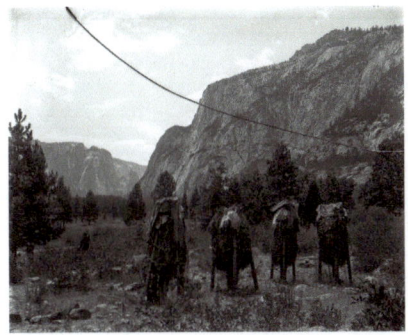 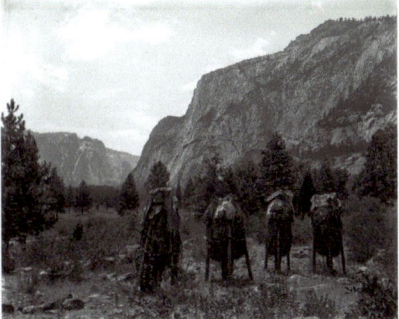

Indian Acorn Cache Before and After Digital Editing

BIBLIOGRAPHY

Bates, Craig D. "The Yosemite Museum Shop: Continuing a Yosemite Tradition," *Yosemite Association Magazine,* Winter 1999.

Coronado Historical Association. "From the Vault: Harold Taylor Collection," *Field Notes.* https://coronadohistory.org/blog/from-the-vault-harold-taylor-collection-slide-44/ (accessed July 2022).

Ditton, Richard P. and Donald E. McHenry. *Self-guiding Auto Tour of Yosemite National Park.* 1956. http://www.yosemite.ca.us/library/auto_tour/wawona.html (accessed July 2022).

Elliott, Betty Jewel. Letter to the Coronado Chamber of Commerce, February 20, 1985.

Elliott, William T. Notes from personal communications with Robert Elliott. Late 1980s.

Epting, Chris. *Teddy Roosevelt in California.* The History Press. 2015.

Encyclopedia Britannica. "History of Photography." https://www.britannica.com/technology/photography/Photographys-early-evolution-c-1840-c-1900 (accessed July 2022).

Fiske, George. "Yosemite Valley. From Inspiration Point," Getty Museum Collection. https://www.getty.edu/art/collection/object/104M92 (accessed July 2022).

Harrison, Steve. "Photographers from on High: Arthur Pilsbury's Yosemite," *Yosemite Association Magazine.* Summer 1996.

National Park Service. "History and Culture," *Yosemite National Park.* 2022. https://www.nps.gov/yose/learn/historyculture/index.htm

NorCal Hiker. "Inspiration Point, Artist Point, and the Old Wawona Road," *NorCal Hiker.* July 22, 2013. http://www.norcalhiker.com/inspiration-point-artist-point/

Russell, Carl P. "Early Years in Yosemite," *California Historical Society Quarterly.* December 1926. http://www.yosemite.ca.us/library/early_years_in_yosemite/ (accessed July 2022).

Smaus, Louis H. "The Artists & Photographers of Yosemite (1855-1935)," *Yosemite Association Magazine.* Winter 1987.

Taylor, Harold A. Letter to Ralph H. Anderson, Yosemite National Park Archives. November 18, 1949.

United States Geological Survey. "Geological Sketch of the Yosemite Region and the Sierra Nevada," *Geological Survey Professional Paper 160.* 2006. https://www.nps.gov/parkhistory/online_books/geology/publications/pp/160/sec1e.htm

Wikipedia. "Richard Leach Maddox." April 7, 2022. https://en.wikipedia.org/wiki/Richard_Leach_Maddox

Yosemite National Park Archives. "Leases In Yosemite Valley." 1905.

INDEX

Acorn Cache   14, 141
Adams, Ansel   1
Alabama Tree. See Most Perfect Tree
Artist Point   7, 8, 9
Ayres, Thomas   8
Bachelor and Three Graces   117, 118, 119
Best, Harry   1
Boysen, Julius   1
Bridalveil Fall   7, 11, 32, 33, 34, 35
Bridge   66, 72, 82, 83
Butler, Nicholas Murray   91
Cabin   104, 105, 106, 107, 108, 109, 110
California Tree   127
Camp Curry   1
Carriage   90, 96, 97, 98, 99, 107, 115, 116, 131
Cascade Falls   36
Cathedral Peak   68
Cathedral Rocks   7, 17, 55, 81
Cathedral Spires   49, 50, 51, 81
Cedar Tree   18
Chapel   2
Clark, Galen   1, 123
Clouds Rest   7, 71
Columbia Tree   122
Commissioners Trees   112, 113
Confederate Group   120, 121
Cook's Meadow   16
Creek   72, 73, 74, 77, 78, 79
Crescent Lake   84, 85
Diamond Group   133
Dome   7, 8, 46, 47, 48, 56, 57, 61, 62, 63, 64, 65, 66, 67, 77
El Capitan   7, 39, 40, 41
Elliott   xv, 139, 140
Faithful Couple Trees   129
Fallen Monarch   96, 97

Fiske, George   1, 9
Foley, Daniel J.   1
Four Mile Trail   23, 24, 55
Gates of the Valley   10, 11, 12
Glacier Point   1, 23, 24, 55, 57, 58, 59, 60, 61, 63
Glass Plate Negatives   1, 139, 140, 141
Governor Gene Todd Group   114, 115, 116
Governor Tree   111, 112, 113
Grizzly Giant   89, 90, 91, 92, 93, 94, 95
Half Dome   7, 57, 61, 62, 63, 64, 65, 66, 67
Hallett, Eugene   1, 2
Happy Isles   2, 46, 47, 80
Haverford Tree   110
Hawaiian Islands Trees   128
Haymaking   16, 17
Indian   1, 14, 15, 141
Inspiration Point   8, 9
Lake   67, 68, 71, 75, 76, 84, 85
Leidig Meadow   17
Loeb Jr, William   91
Longfellow Tree   131
Lost Arrow Trail   77
Maddox, Richard Leach   139
Mariposa   33, 123
Massachusetts Tree   122
Merced River   11, 81, 82, 83
Minnow Lake   85
Mirror Lake   75, 76
Moody, William H.   91
Moran Point   10
Most Perfect Tree   126
Mt. Conness   67
Mt. Watkins   76

145

Muir, John   1, 91
Nevada Fall   31
North Dome   8, 46, 47, 48
Oak Trees   13
Ohio Tree   110
Old Guard, The   124
Overhanging Rock   58, 59, 60
Pardee, Governor George C.   91
Photographer's Rock   57
Pillsbury, Arthur C.   2
Ranger   89, 90, 94, 98
Rhode Island Tree   105
River   11, 49, 65, 81, 82, 83
Rixey, Dr. Presley M.   91
Road   26, 27, 33, 44, 50, 75, 102, 103, 132, 133, 134
Roosevelt, President Theodore   1, 91
Royal Arches   8, 48
San Diego Tree   125
Sentinel Dome   7, 8, 56
Sentinel Rock   2, 7, 53, 54, 55
Stanford Point   9
Stream   78, 79
Studio of the Three Arrows   xv, 1, 2, 3
Study   72, 73, 74, 102, 103, 132, 133
Sunset Tree   130
Taft Point   52
Taylor, Harold   xv, 1, 2, 7, 18, 33, 123, 139, 140
Telescope Tree   120
Tenaya Canyon   64, 67
Tenaya Creek   72, 73
Tenaya Lake   67, 68, 71
Three Brothers   42, 43, 44
Tis-sa-ack   62
Trail   19, 23, 24, 26, 27, 55, 63, 77
Tunnel View   7, 8
Vermont Tree   100, 101, 102, 103
Vernal Fall   30
Wagon   10, 16, 17, 50
Washburn Point   61, 62, 63
Washington Column   45, 48

Wawona   2, 7, 33, 84, 85
Wawona Tree   98, 99, 100, 101, 102, 139
Wheeler, Benjamin Ide   91
Whittier Tree   131
William McKinley Group   121
Yosemite Creek   77, 78, 79
Yosemite Falls   16, 23, 24, 25, 26, 27, 29
Yosemite Fall, Upper   28
Yosemite Valley   xv, 1, 2, 7, 13, 123

www.ingramcontent.com/pod-product-compliance
Lightning Source LLC
Chambersburg PA
CBHW040216220526
45473CB00001B/6